My Journey:

Pre-War to post-Covid

Wendy Billington

Grosvenor House
Publishing Limited

This book is published by
Grosvenor House Publishing Ltd
Link House
140 The Broadway, Tolworth, Surrey, KT6 7HT.
www.grosvenorhousepublishing.co.uk

A CIP record for this book
is available from the British Library

ISBN 978-1-80381-624-1

My Journey: Pre-war to post-Covid

Shaped today through experiences of yesterday

Wendy Billington

To my fellow travellers

PART 1

Contents

Preface

Over the last 80 years there have been two global episodes of major significance, each of which have adversely affected the everyday lives of countless people: a worldwide conflict and a devastating pandemic. I was just eight years of age when the Second World War was declared. Then in the early spring of 2020 the coronavirus arrived and began to spread across our country. Both these major events brought serious disruption to life and a genuine fear of the unknown, with mental instability affecting all age groups.

Along with many others, WW2 deprived me of my formative childhood years, seriously disrupted my education and affected me in my later years, way beyond childhood. Aged 14, I emerged from the war to face the emotional complexities of adolescence. Many youngsters are suffering in similar ways today following the pandemic and it is this that has prompted me to reflect on my wartime experiences, which have lain dormant in me for decades but are still indelibly imprinted on my mind.

During the war, many children living in vulnerable areas were evacuated and accommodated with families who were obliged to open their homes—in some cases reluctantly—as hosts to the evacuees. When the air raid sirens sounded, school lessons were interrupted as the pupils went speedily, but in an orderly manner, to take cover in air raid shelters.

In some parts of the country exams were jeopardised; some took place in the air raid shelters and, in some instances, they were cancelled altogether.

The war was not a time to play party politics as happens now. Wartime Britain was run by a coalition government of predominantly Conservative, Liberal and Labour politicians. Far from being resented, the government's interventions and active interest in providing for the welfare of its people was welcomed by most British citizens.

I recall that, through rationing, there was a fair distribution of food. Particular attention was given to children's nutritional needs, ensuring that we had half a pint of milk a day and were provided with rose hip syrup and cod liver oil to boost our vitamin intake and immune system. During one of my periods of evacuation I played my part by collecting rose hips at weekends. Tirelessly but willingly, young and old contributed to the 'war effort' alongside neighbours and their wider communities.

As I reflect on my experiences of life during the war, comparing them with the coronavirus, I now have an urge to write about my memories of life as a whole over these 90 years. Life has proved to be an interesting one and worth recording. It has had its ups and downs, joys and sorrows, as well as regrets (many of my own making). In a recent sermon based on Psalm 85 the words 'love and faithfulness' are still ringing in my ears. As a Christian, I do not regret these experiences knowing that, by God's providence, they have shaped my future. Truly, my loving and faithful heavenly

Father has always been there for me. I have neglected and failed him time and time again but I know he has never abandoned me; he forgives me and puts me on this path of life again, giving me the strength to press on.

At the end of each chapter of Part One of this book, I write about my journey of faith. Some of those reading my story may have little or no faith, so I hasten to add that my faith has been severely battered over the years, almost to extinction. Now in my latter years I have emerged with many regrets, but with a faith that is as strong as it has ever been.

I lost my only sister Mary very recently. She was four years my senior. Mary and Hugh (my brother-in law, who died two years before) lived in Sevenoaks in the same house for 50 years, less than a mile from where I now live. For a number of years, they both lived in Riyadh, Saudi Arabia, where Hugh played his part as a quantity surveyor in the building of the King Faisal Hospital. Although so different in temperament and the contrasting routes our lives have taken, the loss of Mary and Hugh has left a gap in my life— much larger than expected.

Mary dabbled in writing too. Shortly after her death a short, factual autobiography written in 2006 was found. It is beautifully written and in her own handwriting—not a word erased, altered or crossed out. I am delighted that parts of her account seem so relevant to my own reflections, so I want to include them in my own story.

Introduction

My mother was 33 years of age and my father 49 when I was born. I was totally ignorant of their age difference until I was well into my teens, when it came as a shock to be told that my father was approaching the great age of 70. Although he had valvular heart problems during WW1 that prevented him from joining up, and flu in the 1919 epidemic, he had, as I was constantly told, 'no health problems; he was still working'. Although he suffered a limp over many years and used a stick, he walked everywhere he could and seemed to me to be in his prime. He was a journalist totally dedicated to his work and career. Having moved from Wales to Sidcup shortly after the end of WW1, he took up the post of reporter of a large local newspaper, the *Kentish Times*; subsequently he became editor of the *Eltham Times* and during WW2 acted as correspondent for national newspapers. Our house was strewn with these newspapers on a daily basis because, much to my mother's consternation, my father was a hoarder. He was much loved and valued by the public and completely bipartisan in his reporting. He loved what he did and lived for his work, sometimes to the detriment of family life. However, I was always proud of him and all he achieved. I would have gladly followed in his footsteps and had a career in journalism but sadly that wasn't to be. My father was a 'people' person, as I am; he just loved and lived for his work.

My mother was also a career person and I think she secretly regretted giving up a very promising post with the United Nations in Geneva to marry my father, Taffy. Yes, he *was* a Welshman with a Welsh accent! She told me that she wanted to get back to her work just as soon as she could after I was born when my sister was in all-day education. It was thus a daytime nanny called Dorothy, living just across the road, who came to look after me every day, except on Friday when my father took over for the day.

Mummy, as I called her, was always juggling her life between motherhood and her career. She was private secretary to a financier, Francis Hill Cole, who lived in Knightsbridge; Mary and I thought she had a secret love for him and he for her, but that we couldn't ask her! Subsequently, Mummy worked in the city as a personal assistant to two financiers.

The first was Sir Denys Lowson, a barrister, who became lord mayor of London in 1951, the year of the Festival of Britain. I was led to understand that he was the youngest, richest and most controversial lord mayor there has ever been! Mother didn't really enjoy working for him, saying he was 'conceited and pompous'; she told me he had his own photo on the back of his loo door! His ambitious nature and thirst to make money was his eventual downfall and led to his early tragic death. I am not sure whether Mother actually wrote his speech for the Lord Mayor's Banquet in 1951, but I do know that she was still typing it as he was sitting down in his place of honour and that she handed it to him over his shoulder whilst he was eating, shortly before he was due to deliver it.

The other financier, Alan Hanbury, was by far the more honourable and of a pleasant nature; she worked for him over many years.

Mine was a home birth, delivered by my mother's friend who was a midwife. It was also a particularly agonising one, a fact that my mother often recounted when I was naughty! Mary was four at the time and attending a nursery school. My arrival apparently disturbed the peace and equilibrium of the household.

Mary and I were like chalk and cheese. Only in later years have I been able to identify similarities. She was quiet, seemingly unemotional, tidy and highly organised, instinctively well-behaved and courteous, accepting all that came her way. However hard I tried, I was somewhat untidy (taking after my father), emotional and impetuous. I had such a love of life and, as a youngster, I was so proud that I lived only 12 miles from the capital of the greatest country in the whole world! I recall times when my father would take my hand and we would saunter together into the garden after dusk to gaze at the sky and the countless stars. As a little one I was mesmerised by the vastness of the universe and, even at a young age, I started to wonder how it came into existence.

I am aware and appreciative that I was well brought up. Mother taught me to adhere to the rudiments of good behaviour and courtesy. For instance, I would be reprimanded if I knew a person's name and didn't use it when talking to them, and to look into their face and not at the ground. As an emotional person, I was oozing love for others but at the same time craving that love for myself. I longed for cuddles but, as far as I can remember, there were few.

For the first six years of my life, I lived in a small, cosy bungalow in Sidcup. My father had a den at the back of our living room where he spent many hours each day writing up events and articles for his treasured *Kentish Times*. Towards the end of the day, he would take the day's copy to his main office less than ten minutes' walk away. Most evenings he would be out, in his reporting role, attending local events. In a nutshell, we saw very little of him.

When my mother returned to work, I was two and Mary was just starting all-day education at a small prep school in a house nearby. The *Kentish Times* went to press on a Thursday evening, so Daddy was encouraged to take Friday as his regular day off. Friday became Dorothy's day off as well, which meant Daddy could look after me. I had him all to myself! I simply loved our special times together. Fridays would often include a visit to the WH Smith bookstall on the 'Up' platform of Sidcup station where I was treated to an 'approved' comic or a youngsters' newspaper.

On the other four weekdays, I was in the care of Dorothy, who always came wearing her uniform of a green overall. Mother was insistent that Dorothy arrived on time and left on time. As soon as Dorothy knocked on the door in the morning, my mother was off to the station. When Mother arrived back in the evening Dorothy had to be off home! I liked Dorothy but was too young to remember what we did together except go for walks. Quite likely we would do a bit of household shopping together.

Weekends were special as Mother was home and Father would normally be free of work on Sundays. Mother was very hospitable and she had a number of close friends living in London who would be invited for Sunday lunch or occasionally arrive on Saturday to spend the weekend with us.

As a special treat when Daddy was home on Sundays, and knowing how much it meant to me, just before bedtime he might take me into the garden to see the beauty of the night sky.

The heavens declare the glory of God
and the sky above declares his handiwork. (Psalm 19 v1)

CHAPTER 1

Glimpses into Early Childhood, 1931–1939

First Episode

My Mother writes: *I returned from London one Friday evening with a spring in my step—I was looking forward to my cousin Queenie's visit that Sunday. There was a downside to her visits as for some reason Wendy threw a tantrum almost as soon as Queenie came through the door. I only hope this won't happen again for, to say the least, it was all so embarrassing for me and discourteous to Queenie, who is her godmother. Surely at three I should be able to control her. I and Taffy have brought up both Wendy and Mary to be well-behaved, particularly when friends and relatives such as Auntie Queenie are around. There is some consolation in knowing that Mary is so different; she wouldn't dream of wanting to behave in this way.*

It was shortly after midday on that Sunday morning when Queenie arrived with Taffy, who had met her at the station. There were the usual greetings with a peck on the cheek, the handing over by Queenie of the customary gift of a box of chocolates followed by her disappearance to wash her hands.

With these preliminaries over we all, except Wendy, went into the living room where the coal fire was burning merrily in the hearth and Taffy was waiting with sherry and glasses. Through all of this Wendy had been hovering around in the background in the hall and her bedroom; her sulky facial expression told it all. Taffy poured out the sherry for the three of us with an orange juice for Mary; taking mine into the kitchen I continued the final preparations for lunch. And then it started. First, I heard a quiet grizzle followed by sobbing that seemed to turn into loud seemingly uncontrollable crying.

I had had enough so in anger I dragged and flung Wendy into her bedroom room, telling her that unless she stops crying, she will stay there until Queenie leaves after teatime. I do recall that when lunch was being served Taffy did sneak into the room, taking her some lunch.

This event was one of my very earliest memories and has lain almost dormant in my mind until now. As to whether my mother or even Queenie herself understood the reason for my behaviour I have no idea. I never asked. In fact, I could not bear to look at Auntie Queenie because she was so huge compared with others; my reaction was involuntary. She held nothing against me for my conduct and she always gave me Christmas and birthday presents. In my late teens she and I met on a number of occasions and would enjoy a lunch or tea together, often in a cafe on the rooftop of Derry and Toms in Kensington High Street—the store with a station as it was called. I would babble away, as I was prone to do with family and friends, feeling totally at my ease.

Second Episode

We had just moved from our bungalow into a three-storey Victorian semi-detached house in another part of Sidcup. I loved our new home and its spaciousness. Almost from the first day, I would rush around like a whirlwind running up and down the 13 stairs of our first flight, often jumping with a thud the last four steps. One of many 'weaknesses', as my mother called them, was that of always rushing, something that I am still prone to do 80 years on but, suffice it to say, at a slower rate!

One day the inevitable happened. Halfway down the stairs, I slipped and fell, landing in a heap at the bottom, and began screaming loudly for help from my mother, who was upstairs at the time. Silence! No response!

I had fallen. I was in pain. I was in shock. Did my mother not care? I began to scream all the more loudly and urgently: 'Quick, quick, Mummy. I'm dead!' That should work, I thought. Even then it was a few minutes before she actually appeared with a disgruntled look on her face. Was her delay deliberate? I will never know. What I surmise is that although I didn't deliberately fall, having fallen I just wanted a cuddle and a bit of attention. Our family didn't do cuddles.

Third Episode

Unlike others we knew, money in our family was a bit short. There was enough for everyday life and a two-week holiday on the Isle of Wight but it was hard-earned by both our parents, with little left for so-called treats. Quite out of the blue, in the early summer of 1937, I was told we were to have a foreign holiday in France in late August. Arrangements had been made to go with Mummy's brother Cyril and his wife Hetty (who was Belgian by birth and French speaking), together with their two children for a fortnight's stay in an annexe of a hotel in the small village of Bernevàl on the outskirts of Dieppe. We were to travel by train to Newhaven, from where we would take a ferry to Dieppe. I remember my excitement at the prospect not just of the holiday but the experience of going abroad and crossing the English Channel—a distance of 58 miles, which took four hours.

The sea was calm and I wasn't seasick, but no-one would have envisaged that halfway across I had a panic attack, likely to have been caused by agoraphobia. A fear washed over me. Wherever I looked there was no land—just water! It is a feeling I will never forget. (Maybe my fear of heights is associated with this event.) Upon arrival at Dieppe, I had an acute ill-timed diarrhoea attack. A great start for the holiday!

It was a holiday to be remembered. The extensive menu was like something from another world. I learned by heart the succession of courses that formed our main meal each day: soup, fish, meat, cheese, dessert and coffee!

A small roof covered the annexe leading into the grounds. Here, I created a shop which I opened every morning after breakfast. All the family would dutifully file in for their purchases, from which I proudly acquired a pocket full of French francs. It was certainly great fun!

Running down the steep hill on which the hotel was situated was also great fun. With my parents' chorus of 'Careful, careful!' ringing in my ears, I loved to run down that hill... until I had a near fatal fall! I screamed and screamed. I was good at that! A huge bump appeared on my forehead, the likes of which I had never seen before nor since. No-one seemed unduly alarmed and it was my father who was allocated the task of giving my head cold compresses throughout the rest of the day.

For me this was an eventful and memorable holiday. Not long after, in 1942, that same village of Bernevàl experienced a devastating tragedy. On the very beach where we had played as children only five years earlier, the Canadian Army launched an unfortunate and ill-prepared invasion. As the Canadian soldiers made their way up the hill, their enemy was waiting. They had no chance of survival. The Canadian force suffered huge casualties with hundreds killed and thousands wounded or taken prisoner.

Fourth Episode

It was all a bit 'hush hush' at first. In June 1939, my mother and I went to see Dr Bernard about a small lump that had appeared in my groin. There was no National Health Service in those days; a doctor's consultation fee was two guineas. I still remember and can visualise the confidential chat in the doctor's room between Dr Barnard and my mother whilst I waited out of earshot at the other end of the room. I learned that I needed a hernia operation. I was to be a patient at our local cottage hospital and, following the operation, there would be a recuperation period of three weeks still at the hospital! I have no idea if this had to be paid for but I assume it was.

I have an unusually vivid recollection of my stay in hospital. I was left by my parents in the care of a nurse to face the operation on my own, but I was kept in the dark as to what the operation involved. Looking back now, it must have been so hard for my parents to leave me and not be by my side to hold my hand and give me the love and support I must desperately have needed. This experience is likely to be similar for those needing hospital treatment for Covid when many were left on their own, not knowing what the outcome might be.

The anaesthetic used was ether. It was a ghastly experience, which I remember to this day. A mask was put over my face and, reassured by Dr Barnard, who was to perform it, I was told I would shortly be asleep. Whether the procedures went wrong or not I have no idea; my memory is that of being in a circle which was uncannily and endlessly spinning, first one way and then, with a bang, back round the other way. I had the feeling that I was not in the real world at all but somewhat detached from it. I experienced this feeling of detachment frequently in the weeks that followed and I do so very occasionally even today.

Apparently, it is somewhat unusual for a female and someone so young to have a hernia lump in the groin. The operation was successful and prevented the life-threatening complication of a strangulated hernia. I am still the proud owner of the long scar in my left groin.

I was only allowed an occasional visit from my parents. However, dear Daddy turned up trumps and did all he could to look after me, leaving a present such as a comic, books or puzzles at the hospital most days, writing me regular letters and showing real concern. What is more, he apparently wrote a brief article about my spell in the hospital in the local paper, focussing on my bravery! I was not too happy about this publicity but had no choice in the matter. That was just typical of him and his love of writing.

Three weeks after the operation, when I was eventually told I could get out of bed, I discovered it was almost impossible to walk! Nobody told me that my muscles would be weak. Nobody prepared me for not being able to walk!

Then, when I was discharged from the hospital, I was warned not to run for the next two or three months. For a lively eight-year-old that struck me as hard indeed, especially as our annual family holiday to the Isle of Wight was two months later, at the end of August.

CHAPTER 2

The Beginnings of War,
1939–1940

For my sister who was twelve and I eight the word *surreal* could have aptly described the tense atmosphere that we felt pervading the air on that sunny early September Sunday morning in 1939. Neither of us wanted to add to the obvious anxieties of our parents at that time so, like everyone else, we quietly accepted what was happening that day, restraining ourselves from verbalising what might have been going on inside our minds.

We were staying on the Isle of Wight in the delightful seaside resort of Bembridge. My godmother, Auntie Hilda, had been invited to join our family as she had for previous holidays. The threat of war had been hanging over us for a couple of years but during the previous few months it was becoming more of a reality. Our annual family holiday—the highlight of the year for Mary and me—had been in jeopardy. Conscious of the disappointment that cancelling the holiday would cause us, my parents decided to go ahead with it.

There was high excitement in the week leading up to our departure. As with previous holidays, a trunk had been carefully packed and a card left in our front room window to alert Carter Paterson, a rail haulage company owned by the Big Four railways, that we had an item to be collected for delivery. With the paperwork completed and signed and the trunk taken away, we had total confidence that our trunk would be awaiting us upon arrival in our rented bungalow four days later. And it was! (The year before lockdown, I discovered that a similar service existed. I made good use of it when I stayed on the south coast of France. Well worth it when of older years!)

Also awaiting us was Auntie Hilda. She and our mother were close friends and had known each other since they first started school in 1904. She lived in Ealing in west London and was one of our frequent weekend guests.

On that Sunday morning, just over a week into our holiday, we made our way as a fivesome from our beach hut to an assembly point further along the beach, each clutching a folding chair. We made sure we were in good time. At 11 o'clock the prime minister, Neville Chamberlain, was due to make a special announcement to our nation on the radio. Had he been able to avert war? That was the question that was uppermost on our lips. We sat down on our chairs in orderly rows, eager yet apprehensive about what we were due to hear. We knew that nothing short of a miracle, it would be bad news.

Soon after we heard Big Ben strike 11 o'clock, the voice of the prime minister came across over the radio relayed to us all through a loudspeaker. We learned that Adolf Hitler had been given the opportunity by Chamberlain to withdraw German troops from Poland—a country they had invaded two days earlier—but he had stubbornly refused to do so. We then heard loud and clear: 'This country is at war with Germany.'

For people like my parents, who had each experienced the horrors of WW1, the prospect of yet another war just two decades on must have been, to say the least, shattering for them. The joys of parenthood were now to be overshadowed by the burden of responsibility and protection of those who were dear to them. To have borne a child into a world at war with the implications of suffering and privation, no parent would relish.

After the announcement that we were at war, we were told that there were respirators (gas masks) waiting for distribution. These were to be carried at all times. I had noticed the massive boxes to the right of where we were sitting and wondered what they might contain. Now I knew. Unlike most children in those times, I longed to be part of the adult world. The make-believe world of dolls and prams was not for me, so I hoped I would not be given a Mickey Mouse gas mask. I wanted an ordinary adult one. Mary was totally different from me, entering into that make-believe world with great enthusiasm.

We were asked to file in alphabetical order of surnames. As our name was Saunders, we were a little way down the list. When my turn came to collect my mask, it was such a relief to discover there were no Mickey Mouse ones left! We spent a while practising putting them on, which I seemed to find more difficult than other children there. I lacked, and do still lack, a measure of dexterity; something that frustrated me and irritated my mother! The masks had a horrid smell of rubber. I have learned only recently that the gas masks contained asbestos, which today is a forbidden material as it can create a serious and often lethal lung condition known as asbestosis. A dear friend died from this condition a short while ago, having been exposed to asbestos in the course of his working life.

We made our way back to our beach hut knowing a decision needed to be made: should we curtail our holiday and go home, or stay on until the Friday when our fortnight's holiday was due to end? I longed to stay on! After much deliberation, Auntie Hilda decided she would return to her home. Our father offered to accompany her to Ealing before returning home himself.

Mary writes: *My father was a journalist on the* Kentish Times *and he seemed to work all day, every day except Fridays, when the paper had been published the previous evening. He was highly respected for his writings, courtesy and for the sympathetic way in which he dealt with sensitive material. All his 'copy' was handwritten, often sitting on his bed and taken to the office each day in Sidcup, a task which I would undertake occasionally.*

Father would have seen it as his duty to return to his work. Mother was conscious of the dangers of bombing and was reluctant at the time to return to our hometown of Sidcup, which was considered quite vulnerable to attack since it was only 12 miles south-east of central London. After further deliberation between our parents, there was a whip round for coins in order to make a long-distance call from the nearby telephone kiosk. Following that mystery call, we were told that Mother's friend, Auntie Alice, had invited us to stay a while with her in High Wycombe. Arrangements were made for the three of us to travel there at the end of our holiday the following Friday.

I was delighted we were staying on to finish our holiday, but my heart sank at the thought of staying with Auntie Alice. She had been a lodger with Mother's parents during WW1 and I was aware that whatever the reason it had not turned out too well. Time would tell!

Soon it was time to pack our trunk and arrange for its despatch with one remaining suitcase to be packed to take with us. I cannot recall the details of that journey. In order to avoid London, it needed careful planning, but that certainly would not have daunted Mother.

And so began our first evacuation!

Auntie Alice lived in a comfortable, detached house a mile or so from High Wycombe's town centre. I had been told that she was 'well off'. I can remember very few positive things about our time with Auntie Alice but vividly recall two negatives.

One of these was her frugality with food. At that point in the war, there was no food rationing nor need of it.

Nevertheless, her ruling was that Sunday's roast had to last until Friday. The servings on our plates were quite pathetic compared with what we were used to at home. We did not complain but hid our actual thoughts and feelings, including the empty feeling of rumbling tums!

The other negative occurred on our second night there. Naturally, we were tired from our journey when we arrived on the Friday, so after a 'lick and a promise', we were soon sound asleep in our beds. However, on the second night it wasn't quite the same. Auntie Alice offered to put me to bed. This would have been a totally new experience for her. Aged eight, I was relatively independent and was used to getting ready for bed on my own. I would normally call to Mother once I was in bed and then, after a special chat together and sometimes a story, I would be tucked up and kissed 'goodnight'. I remember, as clearly as if it were yesterday, that Auntie hovered around, ill-at-ease, as I washed; when I was about to get into bed, she insisted that I knelt down by my bed to say my prayers, something I had never done before in someone else's presence. Prayers, if they were said at all, were totally private between me and God! I stubbornly refused!

I have no idea what happened next but I know I was desperately upset and totally unable to handle the situation, feeling guilty, embarrassed and ashamed, unable to share what had occurred with anyone. Although I had always believed in God, talking about him with others present was totally alien to me. No doubt Auntie would have found little difficulty in telling my mother of the incident and how remiss it was that she hadn't brought me up to say my prayers each evening at bedtime.

Mother had made prior arrangements for us to meet the headmistress of Wycombe Abbey School on the Monday morning following our arrival, with a view to being admitted as pupils at the start of the school term two days later. It was, and still is, a prestigious school. Looking back now, it was a privilege to be educated there. We were accepted as day pupils. Second-hand uniforms were quickly found for us so that we could start on time.

I loved the school and all that it offered, but continuing there for a longer time had to be weighed against the unhappiness the three of us were experiencing with Auntie Alice. She meant well but it just wasn't working out. Irrespective of where we might live, Mother was also intent on finding a suitable secretarial post, which she needed not just for financial reasons but for her general morale and well-being.

What could Mother do to resolve the situation? As I write now, I am trying to put myself in her shoes. On the positive side we were both happily settling into our new school. We could become boarders but was there enough money to meet the fees? Although Auntie Alice had been kind in giving us accommodation, in retrospect our presence may have been a burden to her, upsetting the equilibrium of her normal life. We could go home to Sidcup, but how safe was it to do so? No doubt, Mother felt quite alone. She had only the two of us with whom she could talk things through.

With the benefit of hindsight, I think she made a wise decision.

Shortly before war was declared, Grandma (mother's mother) had moved from Ealing in west London to live with her brother, Jim, in Chesham, Buckinghamshire. There were a variety of reasons for this; to avoid the dangers of bombing, which were likely in the city, and to facilitate healing for her ulcerated leg. It was felt the fresh air and exposure to the sun in the more rural surroundings would help her leg heal.

Since Chesham was only 12 miles from High Wycombe, it was decided that we would make our own way there the following Saturday and stay overnight. This would give Mother time to talk over our dilemma with both Grandma and Uncle Jim and decide what to do next.

I clearly recall the details of our journey. Neither Mary nor I wanted to be left with Auntie Alice, so it was decided that we would travel with Mother. Our route would take us on three separate buses. However, knowing that the three buses ran quite spasmodically, Mother decided that it would be simpler to walk the first eight miles to Amersham. Then we would find a bus running in the afternoon to take us direct to the gates of Uncle Jim's home. Cutting out the first two bus journeys would help the cash flow problem as Mother seemed to be running out.

Undertaking the long walk to Amersham was a challenge but, even aged eight, I responded well to one as important as this. Auntie Alice was told we were going to Chesham for the weekend to see Grandma. For her sake we knew we needed to be transparent about our plans.

I take my hat off to our mother. She took this initiative and didn't wilt under her responsibilities for her care of us. I am sad that, at the time, we didn't really appreciate her wisdom and resilience. She must have been delighted to see her mother, be welcomed by Uncle Jim and relax and talk with them.

Uncle owned a bungalow on the outskirts of Chesham, on the road to Berkhamsted. 'Hillcrest' was built halfway up Nashleigh Hill and had a most beautifully tiered, sloping garden. Approaching the garden from the bungalow, we negotiated steps, alongside waterfalls and rockeries, which spiralled down to a shaped swimming pool with its changing rooms close by. A tennis court, croquet lawn and even a summer house were all part of the amenities. Not to be forgotten and important for all was the full-time gardener-cum-chauffeur. Beyond the pool, in another direction, were beehives; Uncle was the beekeeper. Mary called Hillcrest 'a paradise' and, for the freedom it gave the two of us, it truly was!

When Uncle Jim realised the imminence of war he had created an air raid shelter—a godsend for us. Attached to the side of the bungalow, it provided comfortable self-contained accommodation all prepared for us and any subsequent visitors that might appear.

Uncle Jim had a Rolls Royce which was his pride and joy. Yes, it is true that he was financially 'comfortably off'. He was of a kind, gentle, humble and generous disposition and had worked tirelessly for many years in a mortgage company he created and from which he had recently retired. I recall that he was quite handsome with a distinguished moustache. I realise now that there was nothing about him that would make someone shy. Nevertheless, I was a bit in awe of him and not always at ease.

It was decided that we would stay on for a few days rather than just one night. Mother would return to High Wycombe to collect our belongings and contact the school to tie up the loose ends there. Mary and I were to stay at Hillcrest to be cared for by Grandma. Mother would explain to Auntie Alice that we were returning home, as it seemed safe to do so. For us, the prospect of being able to lead our normal lives again, as far as the restrictions of the war would allow, came as a relief.

I remember that the weather for late September was in our favour, and those few days were spent enjoying the delights and facilities of the garden with the novelty of staying in the air raid shelter on our own but with Grandma and Uncle nearby to call on if need be.

A few days after Mother had returned from High Wycombe to Chesham, we returned home by train. Uncle Jim's chauffeur-cum-gardener took us to Chalfont station and then we travelled onward by train, via London, back to our home in Sidcup.

Suffice it to say this was a short-lived evacuation for us at the start of the war, but nonetheless interesting, eventful and an experience that has remained clearly in my memory over the decades. Our return home would have coincided with the start of the second half of the Christmas term, a convenient time to re-start school.

Father must have been relieved to have us back and for our lives to return to some normality, or perhaps we should call it a 'new normal'. (This can be compared with the recent prospect of a 'new normal' following the lifting of the lockdown from Covid-19, still not knowing what the future might hold.) Father's culinary skills were limited! He could just about boil an egg but not much more. He probably frequented a local cafe for his meals. At that time these were known as 'Community Feeding Centres', but Winston Churchill (who became prime minister one year later) changed the name to 'British Restaurants'. These restaurants, run by the local authority or voluntary agencies, were on a 'not-for-profit' basis. Being the social individual that he was, Father would have enjoyed chatting with local folk there.

I returned to Worcester House, my prep school in Sidcup, just as rumours were circulating that the school was to be evacuated.

It was in 1937 that we had moved into a semi-detached Victorian house, which was in a quiet and pleasant area of Sidcup. Roads there were lined with flowering cherry trees which looked stunning in the springtime. We had five bedrooms, two of which were attic bedrooms, spacious and easily approached by a stairway. They served us well, initially as playrooms but subsequently taken over by our father for his work.

Mary writes: *Returning home, we collected identity cards; my number was CJQW65/3, Wendy's CJQW/4, the 3 and 4 denoting our place in the family. Our gas masks were to be carried everywhere and were contained in a square cardboard box with an assorted number of colours slung round our shoulders.*

Early in 1940 ration books were issued to be registered at Mr Goddard's, our local grocer, and he would be appropriately allocating the food for all the customers registered with him. We were entitled to one egg, 2oz of butter, an adequate amount of tea leaves, 1oz cheese, 8oz sugar, bacon and cooking fats and margarine—the taste of the latter was not pleasant and I tried to avoid it! As children we had a special sweet ration which was more than that of our parents. Mother wanted to be very fair about all our rations and, with Mary's help, she would always give each of us our correct portions. Unlike Mother and me, Father loved having two lumps of sugar in his tea but would often run out and then look nonchalantly into space, knowing that I didn't have a sweet tooth and would take delight in giving him some of mine. We never went hungry as the Ministry of Food ensured that children lived on a healthy diet.

Everyday life was changing. The future was uncertain. As youngsters we were somewhat fearful about what it might hold. In the late summer of 1940, in that first year of the war, fear of the unknown pervaded us all as it has done during the pandemic.

Epilogue

As I look back on that somewhat soul-destroying 'Auntie Alice' episode, I try now to see her in a different light. She had never married, was a strict Baptist and had lived a sheltered life working as a civil servant. With little experience or understanding of young children, it was likely that she didn't feel at ease with youngsters. She probably assumed that most children would be taught to say their prayers at bedtime. I will excuse and forgive her!

As an eight-year-old brought up within a family in which God was rarely mentioned, what faith, if any, did I have? What was the background of faith of my parents?

On my father's side, Grandma Wales, as we called her, had been born in Ireland and brought up a Catholic; Grandpa Wales, born in Sussex, was of Protestant tradition. Living his early years in the small village of Langland Bay, with a population of less than a thousand, Father attended the local school. Over the years I came to realise that at heart Father was comfortable with the higher Anglican church tradition. However, having read some of his newspaper articles written in 1921, his theological views did not quite conform to high Anglican doctrine. With the benefit of hindsight, I know his faith was deep-rooted and he was consistently throughout his life a person of honesty, integrity and of a generous spirit.

On the maternal side my mother had faithfully attended a Wesleyan chapel throughout her childhood. She spent her life searching for the truth and in later life exploring a number of different sects and denominations.

From a young age I know I believed in a Creator God—one who created the universe and me! I recall the joy of going into our attic playroom of an evening and gazing through the window, mesmerised by the wonder of the night sky and in total awe of its beauty and enormity. In mid-February 2021, mission to Mars became a reality when the rover 'Perseverance' landed on the red planet. To me, such a feat was mind blowing. How science and technology have advanced during my lifetime!

At my prep school we had regular school prayers at the start of the day followed by a scripture lesson; I especially loved some of the Bible stories we heard. This, and the Auntie Alice episode, seemed to have little connection with my own belief in an amazing Creator and loving God who I believed created the stars. What hung in the balance was whether my simple belief in this Creator God would remain stagnant or whether it would, in time, develop.

And God made the two great lights—
the greater light to rule the day and
the lesser light to rule the night
and the stars. (Genesis 1 v 16)

CHAPTER 3

Britain Under Threat, 1940–1942

As we entered 1940, there was much that lay in store for our country. We knew that many lives would be affected by this tragic war. As a nine-year-old, I was apprehensive and afraid but I tried to put on a brave face. I longed for peace and the familiar, yet I was keenly aware of the fear that pervaded our country: the fear of invasion by a ruthless enemy.

The phrase 'blood, toil, tears and sweat' is one associated with the start of Winston Churchill's premiership in May 1940. He gave all the encouragement he could muster to the citizens of Great Britain whilst communicating that a difficult time lay ahead. We were to take heart and with everyone's sweat and toil we would eventually win through and be victorious. I hung on to those words.

Looking back now I realise that Mother, although not admitting it to us, was constantly fearful for our safety. Father was something of an enigma. He continued to be totally immersed and absorbed in his work, most nights burning the midnight oil into the early hours with very little sleep.

Shortly before the start of the war, Mother had received a letter from her close schoolfriend, Olive (Auntie Olive to us). It contained an invitation for the three of us, in the event of a war, to spend its duration with her on Long Island, New York, and that she would meet our financial needs. If we were to follow this up it would classify as a private evacuation, requiring legal approval. We knew that there were children already being evacuated to the United States without their parents under an official evacuation scheme.

Mary and I were consulted about the prospect of taking up this invitation and were reassured that as this would be a private evacuation Mother would be able to come as well. We would return home to our dear Father once the war was over. The thought of Father all alone and vulnerable worried me but I tried hard to put it to the back of my mind.

The first step was to obtain an official approval in person from the American embassy. Mother, Mary and I travelled to London and queued up alongside many others at a building in Grosvenor Square, not far from Victoria Station and Buckingham Palace. The long queue and wait required some patience but at last Mother was called to be interviewed, leaving Mary and me in the charge of an official. It was not long before she reappeared with a long and sad face; we realised that the interview had not turned out as she would have wished.

Mary and I were allowed to go, but Mother was told that she could not accompany us. The decision was hers and she was adamant that she would not let us go on our own so that was that! I know I was a wee bit disappointed; the prospect of both the voyage across the Atlantic and actually living in America was exciting, but I was relieved we wouldn't be leaving Father on his own. Was Mother of the same mind…?

A short while later, a liner carrying evacuees was torpedoed in the Atlantic. Now I know that of the 406 people on board, 90 were evacuee children. Of the 258 people who lost their lives, 77 were children.

And so it was that we moved into a world of ration books, blackouts and air raid shelters, and always lurking in our minds was the fear of the unknown and the unexpected. I was adamant: if my school were to be evacuated, I would not be part of it!

Mary writes : *We hung black-out curtains as it was illegal to show a crack of light through the windows, and my mother was actually fined for showing a chink of light from her office window. Air raid wardens (local residents) would be on duty at night to check on this. To prevent splintering of glass, adhesive tape was criss-crossed on windowpanes, many of which we lost several times over due to bomb blast.*

At first, we slept under the stairs, which was considered the safest place, but after a while we went back to our beds, to come downstairs only when the air raid siren sounded.

Later in the war we were to have a cast iron 'Morrison' shelter (named after Herbert Morrison, the home secretary) in the kitchen. It served as a table most of the time but underneath, during the air raids, it was a cosy bed.

During the course of the war, when the nation faced a particular crisis, the king called us to observe National Days of Prayer.

In a national broadcast on 26 May 1940, the king instructed the citizens of the UK to turn back to God and together pray and plead for God's help. That prayer was desperately needed as almost the entire British Army was trapped on the beaches of Dunkerque; Britain was as close as it could be to defeat. People flocked into the churches in their hundreds on that day. Two amazing events then followed. First, a violent storm arose across the Dunkerque coast, grounding the Luftwaffe, who had already been responsible for the killing of thousands on the Normandy beaches. Then a calm arose, allowing hundreds of tiny boats to cross the Channel from England to rescue some 400,000 soldiers. It was seen as nothing short of a miracle such that on 9 June there followed a National Day of Thanksgiving.

Only two months later, when many feared the prospect of an escalating Luftwaffe onslaught in London, a second Day of Prayer was called, followed by yet another on 8 September, precisely one week before the commencement of the Battle of Britain.

The German bombardment of London began with the strategic bombing of the East London docks. The poorer residential areas close to the docks were badly affected, with consequent loss of the lives of civilians.

Sunday, 15 September 1940 is a date that will never be erased from my memory. It was daytime and the skies were clear when we heard the drone of aircraft flying overhead heading for London. We witnessed constant dogfights in the sky above us with planes shot down before our very eyes. Mary writes, *'Barrage balloons hung in the sky to deter low-flying aircraft and as we were close to Biggin Hill we would see the Spitfires coming and going.'*

In their determination to annihilate the RAF and destroy our capital city, the Luftwaffe was launching its largest, most concentrated and ferocious attack on our great city. Their ultimate aim was to force the country into surrender. However, the Spitfire was so designed that it was far superior to the German planes, giving the RAF a definitive advantage over the Luftwaffe.

Our sitting room had a veranda facing north towards the capital. Throughout the day our French doors remained open and we were mesmerised by all that we saw. It began at breakfast time and lasted over 13 hours. It was truly the Battle *for* Britain. As I write reflecting on that day, I have memories of involuntarily shaking from fear, but at the same time being compelled to watch it all. I was particularly fearful not only for ourselves but for the pilots and crew of both the British and the enemy planes; we were witness to some aircraft spiralling out of control and down to earth, with a few escaping by parachute.

As the day progressed and daylight began to fade, we saw the skies ahead of us as one vivid, red glow. Reminiscent of the Great Fire of London in September of 1666, London was burning once more. At the time it was named the Second Great Fire of London, with comparable damage to its historic buildings.

Mary writes: *After our bombers had been on a raid they tried to fly back in formation, usually 12 of them together, and we always hoped that none would be missing.*

At around 7.30 that evening we saw the enemy begin to retreat and limp back to base. Was this yet another answer to prayer? Sadly, some enemy planes off-loaded the residue of their bombs onto the villages and towns over our county of Kent (two of these at least on Sidcup itself) with tragic consequences. We learned of the loss of Mary's closest friend, Olive, and her parents too. The younger daughter, Doreen, aged 10, survived but was now an orphan.

Thanks to the amazing bravery and skill of the RAF pilots and the superior design of the Spitfires they flew, the enemy did not achieve the victory for which it aimed.

Following the events of 15 September 1940, Mother became acutely concerned that the three of us should evacuate, preferably back to the Chesham area, and find somewhere to rent close to where Grandma and Uncle Jim were living. Leaving our father to fend for himself and face the dangers of bombing on his own, once more, was hard and sad.

A few days later, our cases packed with winter clothing, we set off in a taxi towards Chesham, taking a circuitous route in order to avoid London. Our destination was only 30 miles from central London but at least it was away from the bombing.

As we turned right at the end of our road, I recall looking back with sadness and tears in my eyes at leaving our dear Father. It was a profound emotional moment for me, wondering whether we would see him and our home again.

It had been arranged that we would stay with Uncle Jim and Grandma whilst Mother looked for suitable accommodation. So back we were again occupying the same purpose-built, self-contained air raid shelter, with that beautiful garden at our disposal. I knew that there was no escape from needing to continue my education (just as it has been during the lockdown days of the Covid pandemic, when education had to be continued at home), yet I hoped it would not be before half-term! In that interim period Mother searched for a suitable house which we could rent. Her sister-in-law and three children, who also lived in Sidcup, were invited to join us and share the house together.

Mary writes: *After a couple of weeks we found a house to rent and were joined by Auntie Hetty and her children, Jean, Brian and Gillian aged twelve, five and three.*

Auntie Hetty was particularly affected by the bombing; this was understandable as she was Belgian and had lived as a child in Brussels throughout WW1. Mary and Jean were each offered a place at a school evacuated from London to the Royal Masonic School in Rickmansworth and they settled down there well. I started off by attending a local prep school. Sadly, that didn't work out well for me as, although I was with children older than myself, the standard of education was so poor that I learned nothing new as far as the three Rs were concerned. We realised the merits of Worcester House back in Sidcup.

The school's policy was to sit pupils in the classroom in the order of overall achievement. I certainly don't go along with that system now, but looking back I realise that it did bring out the competitive spirit in me and I did well.

During the first four years of school there I had worked hard and had enjoyed it all immensely, leaving with a relatively high level of achievement.

What next? Although the entry age into the grammar school in Rickmansworth was 11 and I was only nine, Mother successfully pleaded for a place for me there. Sadly, it was the start of a downward trend in my education. The quality of the education was not at fault, but quite simply I was too young to be in the school, and too shy to hold my own and cope in that environment.

Mother was offered a post as a personal secretary to a local solicitor. It was a sharp contrast to her working life in London. Although it earned her a reasonable salary, she gleaned very little satisfaction and fulfilment in what she was doing. According to Mother, her boss was 'dull, as was the nature of the work'. However, the job meant that she would normally be home when we returned from school and that was great!

Our journey to school each day was a relatively long one. It involved a walk of over a mile to the station to catch the 7.30 train, changing trains at Chalfont onto the Rickmansworth train and then an uphill walk to the school. I particularly loved the steam train that ran between Chesham and Chalfont. When the train was quite empty on our way home, I would often put my head out of the window, relishing the sensation of the wind blowing into my face and hair.

The winter of 1940/41 was bitterly cold. With an unusually steep climb up the hill to our home, I would often need to stop halfway to sit on a bench, sometimes sobbing with exhaustion, cold and the pain from the chilblains on my toes and fingers.

Father's weekend visits were the highlight of our week. On Fridays he travelled from Baker Street, arriving at Rickmansworth Station where he would put his head out of the window to look for me, as I was looking out for him! We were both so delighted to greet each other. These weekends were such special times for me. If the weather were favourable, the four of us would walk eight miles or so into the beautiful countryside to a child-friendly pub to have lunch.

As I mentioned, during the war at particular moments of crisis the whole country was called to National Days of

Prayer. Sunday, 23 March 1941 was the fourth Day of Prayer and it coincided with one of Father's weekend visits. Mary and I remembered it all so clearly. The country was aware that Hitler was planning to move against Great Britain, although the precise details were not known. Father seemed to have an inkling, or maybe a bit of a premonition about it. He was much involved in the field of politics, always eager to keep us well informed with current affairs. This included keeping us up to date in ways the war was developing, which Father always communicated with an air of optimism.

Father believed in the power of prayer and he suggested that Mary and I accompany him to the service which was to be held at the parish church in Chesham. Mary and I readily agreed. It seemed to us as if the entire population of Chesham was streaming into that service, with an overflow of people listening as it was relayed outside.

We later learned that Hitler had chosen that day for his planned invasion of England from the Atlantic. On that very Sunday, an earthquake erupted in the seabed, sending most of Hitler's waiting fleet off course and forcing him to abandon the invasion. The outline of this event was written by Clement Attlee in an article for the Daily Telegraph in 1944. Was this yet another miracle and answer to prayer? From then onwards Hitler turned his attention away from Britain eastward to an invasion of Russia.

In the context of that National Day of Prayer I want to mention Mr Brown, the 'chocolate man' as we called him!

Who was he? I have no idea! What was he like? Very pleasant and friendly. How did we meet him? He appeared outside the church on that March National Day of Prayer. He approached us and started to talk not just with our father but to Mary and me as well. As we parted company, he drew from his pocket some chocolates and gave them to us. Since sweets and chocolate were rationed, this was an extremely generous gesture. Mary probably had a better recollection of him than I have but she makes no reference to him in her memoirs, although she does give mention to that day saying, 'that we went to church and prayed'. From time to time, we would meet up with Mr Brown outside the church following the Sunday service, which he regularly attended; each time chocolates would appear from his pocket, which is how he became known to us as 'Mr Brown the chocolate man'! I was normally shy with strangers, but he was easy to talk with and I felt at ease with him. Mother, not having met him, thought otherwise! She had been equally alarmed a year or two before when, in all innocence, I told her about being given a lift to school in Sidcup by a passing cyclist!

Apart from Father's visits, a further highlight was getting to know a delightful family living in a detached house at the top of the steep hill just round the corner from where we were living. Quite unexpectedly one of the family called round to our house and invited the three of us for tea. This started a friendship that has lasted until the present day. 'Fluff' Harris, the mother, became friendly with our mother. I made friends with Margaret, who was a year younger than me. I have clear memories of the many games Margaret and I enjoyed together. Margaret's four-year-old sister, Gillian, took exception to the times when Margaret and I would play hopscotch and she was excluded.

'Fluff' kept chickens, so we became well supplied with eggs. At that time our egg ration was one per week, so we were very grateful for the extra eggs. Occasionally 'Fluff' gave us one of their chickens for our Sunday lunch. I did not partake, as the sight of the hens hanging in their greenhouse completely put me off eating chicken. (This aversion continued until my college days a decade later. I was a vegetarian there, mainly because I enjoyed what was on offer but partly because of this chicken episode!)

We didn't see much of Mr Harris, who worked as a surveyor for Buckinghamshire County Council. He was such a quiet, pleasant and gentle Welshman, and I was always pleased when he was around. Sometimes I was invited to join the Harris family for a meal and that was special. They were a truly lovely, hospitable family and a delight to know.

Mother and Fluff kept in close touch for many years. Fluff sadly died many years before our mother. Margaret and I are still in contact, and until the start of the pandemic we were meeting every so often in London for a natter over a meal often in the crypt of St Martin-in-the-Fields, or in the National Gallery restaurant enjoying its views down Whitehall. Lunch might be followed by a visit to an art gallery or museum. Now we keep in touch by phone and birthday and Christmas cards.

Another highlight whilst in Chesham was enjoying the freedom of the garden at Hillcrest at the weekends. I recall one occasion when Uncle Ron, Mother's brother (who served most of the war in Bomber Command with the RAF in Gibraltar) spent a weekend at Hillcrest whilst on leave. He was full of fun and on this occasion he suddenly swept me off my feet and threw me into the swimming pool, despite my screams that I couldn't swim. I was convinced I was going to drown! My screams and pleas didn't seem to bother him. He achieved his purpose and soon I was able to swim!

Mary writes: *I was very happy there* (the school)*, made some good friends, two of whom were Jewish and had a good education.*

The reverse was true for me. I found making friends difficult, probably because of the two-year age difference. This was exacerbated one morning at our morning assembly when out of the blue I was asked by the headmistress to stand up. She singled me out as child of exemplary behaviour and an example to those who were not! I blushed to the roots of my hair and longed for the floor to swallow me up. I began to get bullied so much that one day I was in such a state that I approached a teacher after lunch and told her that I felt ill. I spent the afternoon in sick bay; Mary was instructed to pick me up at the end of the school day. I think the teacher knew the reason but, in those days, no-one took much action to prevent the perpetrators of bullying or to support the victims.

We had daily religious education lessons and frequently our homework was to memorise a Psalm, which we had to write down during the next lesson. I saw that as an opt-out for the teacher, but I remember some of the Psalms to this day, for which I am grateful. The school had numerous facilities for practical lessons such as cookery, laundry and needlework. Mary mentions in her memoirs that we attended a service every Friday afternoon in the chapel, which was a further reminder that we were an evacuated London grammar school needing to share the buildings, classrooms and facilities of the recently built, prestigious Royal Masonic Boarding School.

All the ups and downs of our evacuations came to an end in April of 1942, when my parents decided that it was safe to return home. I was pleased about this but sad to say 'au revoir' to the Harris family and Grandma too, not knowing when we might meet again. Having accumulated so many possessions over the 18 months of our evacuation, we had little option but to travel home by taxi, as we had done for reasons of safety in September 1940 at the peak of the Blitz.

As we approached the end of our road, I recall a wonderful feeling of relief that we were still alive, that our father was also safe and that we were now able to pick up the strands of our former life. Little did we know what would follow a couple of years later.

Epilogue

As I look back now on those seemingly long 18 months of evacuation ending shortly before my eleventh birthday,

I become acutely conscious of the depth of the challenges that were confronting Britain's population of some 50 million citizens. With the death toll rising on all fronts and the fears that surrounded us in Britain, those special calls for National Days of Prayer continued to be apt and meaningful.

In those early years of my life I never doubted that God was the Creator of the universe, of which the beauty of the countryside around us was a part. During that period of evacuation, I loved visiting our delightful park nearby as well as the weekend family walks into the Chiltern Hills along country lanes, across fields, over styles, through woody glens, invariably coming across flocks of sheep chewing the cud. I grew to be enchanted with the natural world of which God, in whom I believed, was so much a part.

I discovered a different facet of the nature of God through school assemblies, the scripture lessons and the one to whom I prayed on that fourth National Day of Prayer in 1941. I was genuinely eager to attend that special service with Mary and our father; I seemed able to relate to the God I met there. I had a sense, in a small but quite profound way, that he was an actual person who was alive and actually cared and loved every individual!

We had prayed from our hearts, pleading with God to guard our country and DO something to protect us from invasion, pleading like children to their parents. When we heard what had happened on the bed of the Atlantic that day and the way invasion was avoided, I had no doubts. It wasn't just a coincidence. God had listened and answered our prayers and brought about this miracle.

I smile to myself as the words from William Cowper's hymn, written nearly 250 years ago, come to mind: 'God moves in a mysterious way, his wonders to perform; he plants his footsteps in the sea and rides upon the storm'.

The grain of a mustard seed was beginning to grow in my life!

It is like a mustard seed,
which is the smallest of all seeds on earth...
Yet when planted, it grows and becomes
the largest of all garden plants.

CHAPTER 4

The Dark Passage of War, 1942–1945

Mercifully there was less intense bombing following our return from evacuation in April 1942. Mary returned to the grammar school at Chislehurst just a short bus journey or cycle ride away. My previous school in Sidcup, Worcester House, had evacuated into the depths of rural Kent. It was suggested that I attend the same school as Mary although it no longer had a junior department for those under 11. Two months short of reaching that age, I was so pleased to be offered a place. There was some deliberation on the part of the headmistress as to which year group I should join. The agreement was finally made that to avoid repeating the year I had already done at Rickmansworth, I would spend the summer term in the second year and then the following academic year I would stay down in that same year and be just one year younger than the rest of the form.

Mother returned to her full-time secretarial work in London with the financier Mr Francis Hill Cole. We still saw very little of our father for he continued to work very hard reporting, writing and editing for the weekly publication of the *Kentish Times*. He seemed to manage on three or four hours of sleep most nights and sometimes his loud snoring could be heard beyond the bedroom walls! I recall he was not too happy to fulfil his duty as an air raid warden. He was on night duty rota which meant keeping watch on the *Kentish Times'* office roof and needing to be wide awake for potential incidents. I cannot recall any details but, knowing him, he would likely have continued to do his writing on the roof whilst trying to overcome his fear of heights!

I would pop in to see Father in his attic room before I left for school when we would have a special *tête à tête* together. Sometimes he would slip a coin into my hand, suggesting that I buy something just for myself. Mary spent much time after school and at weekends in the homes of her school friends. I was a bit of a lone wolf and was unwittingly becoming somewhat of an independent person, developing an introverted personality which contrasted with the bubbly and lively person I had been in my earlier years.

When I returned home after school during the winter months, I was on 'supper and lighting the fire' duties. The first involved preparing the vegetables for our evening meal; the main dish was either Sunday leftovers or something Mother had bought in the City of London in her lunchtime. Occasionally, when my duties were done, I would go down to the station to meet her off her train. Despite the war, train times were reliable (more so than nowadays!). When well-motivated, I have always enjoyed making myself useful. I wanted 'to help others at all times' as the Guide promise is worded. Throughout my life this desire has been deeply rooted in me.

Lighting the fire was a challenge. I would have a firelighter, very few sticks of wood as they were in short supply, and newspaper. Happily, there was no shortage of the latter as we seemed to have every newspaper under the sun delivered for Father each day! Yet despite much puffing and blowing, however hard I tried, I frequently could not get the fire to light. If my puffing yielded little success, I would use the bellows; there might be a glimmer of a flame but if it disappeared my heart would sink since I had no firelighter or sticks left. My frustration was grim. I am not sure whether Mother's spasmodically used and only swear word 'damn' was part of my vocabulary! I remember I wept buckets, praying and pleading to God for help. I so wanted to have the fire merrily burning away when she returned home tired from London—normally around 6 o'clock. Not wanting the fire to defeat me, I would dip into my pocket money, get onto my bike and head to the grocer's to buy a packet of firelighters or further sticks of wood. I rarely confessed to Mother much of this. I would hide the leftover fire lighters for another time.

I liked cycling, and although I know I was a bit wobbly, I enjoyed this means of travelling to school, which was a couple of miles away. I had strict instructions from Mother and promised faithfully that if I heard an air raid siren I would stop instantly, and not hesitate to knock on the door of the nearest house and ask for shelter. This was wartime, when we were at pains to help and protect one another.

Mary writes: *The school we attended had 'Anderson' shelters in the field (named after John Anderson, a member*

of the Cabinet and nicknamed 'Home Front Prime Minister');
these were dugouts lined with corrugated iron panels
and were damp and cold. At home we slept in a Morrison
shelter (named after Herbert Morrison, the home secretary)
in the kitchen. This was made of cast iron, the top serving as
a table and the underneath as a cosy bed.

At the time, Mary's hobby was collecting bomb shrapnel pieces often found on the pavements of our road. She kept these in a special cupboard on our attic floor. To her they were precious, tangible memories of those war years. She was devastated when we learned that Mother, when clearing that cupboard, had thrown them away.

In June 1944 life changed for the worse. We experienced the first V1 missiles aimed at London. These were the pilotless, two-engine bomber aeroplanes which had a very distinctive frightening rasping *'woo'* sound. Consequently, they were called buzzbombs. It was so very frightening to wait for that monotonous low-pitched drone sound to cut out, followed by an eerie silence as the plane with explosives on board made its descent to earth; we wondered who the victims might be. It still haunts me even today when I hear a plane overhead with a similar distinctive sound. These German V1s were made and launched from the French and Dutch coasts. They had a pre-determined distance to travel but were never able to be programmed accurately to land on a specific target. I have learned subsequently that there were many injuries and deaths in the process of making these rockets.

A V1 actually made a direct hit on a house in a road 100 yards away from ours, destroying it completely and killing the sole resident. Our Victorian house and a number of our neighbours' houses suffered much damage. Time and time again, we would spend the early mornings, along with our neighbours, clearing debris from fallen ceilings and broken windows. We were always thankful that we had been protected from a direct hit.

Father, in his role as a correspondent for some national newspapers, was regularly required to report on incidents in our local area. It meant more work but it was work he enjoyed. Sometimes he asked me to be the courier, which meant taking the copy to Sidcup station and handing it to the guard on the platform of the next train to Charing Cross. Then, having been alerted that the copy was on the train, a courier from Fleet Street would collect and deliver it to the appropriate newspaper office. Father would be quick on the scene to report local incidents and tragedies, bitterly exposing himself to danger. His total absorption in his work probably absorbed his own fears; his love and empathy for others motivated him in all he did—such a contrast and often absent in the average journalist of today. All that said, it was always a relief when we heard his key in the latch and we knew he was safe.

The first of these V1s dropped on Swanscombe in west Kent on 13 June 1944, just a few days after D-Day; the last V1 fell on Orpington three miles from Sidcup on 27 March 1945, less than two weeks before the end of the war. During that period, it is estimated that 6,725 V1s were launched on Britain, nearly half of which targeted London.

D-day and the Normandy landings took place on the 6 June 1944, the day before my thirteenth birthday. My sister's seventeenth birthday was six days later on 13 June, when she was officially notified that she could now be called up for Active National Service. She was already an active member of the Girls' Training Corps, which focused its attention on young people. They were prepared to serve their community, available for support when required. This was her 'war effort' and it meant so much to her to serve in this way. She mentions in her memoirs that she qualified to wear a smart forage cap!

In the weeks and months to follow, I avidly read the newspapers and listened to the radio about the progress of troops following the D-Day landings in Normandy. At first it was mortifying to learn of the loss of life and the slow progress of the troops as they struggled to conquer Caen, but it was exhilarating to learn of the advances which followed. These Allied landings on the beaches of Normandy were the start of a long and costly campaign to liberate north-west Europe from Nazi occupation.

For those of us in Britain, worse was to follow. Early that September the first V2 was launched. Could this actually be seen as the start of the space age which I had read about in the newspapers? These were rockets 14 metres high, containing a tonne of explosives and travelling at lightning speed with no warning before impact.

Let me describe the devastation that just one V2 caused. It happened in New Cross, on the outskirts of London, nine miles from where we lived. It was a busy Saturday lunchtime in November when, with no warning, a silent V2 rocket hit a Woolworth's store. The destruction resembled a battlefield with people thrown into the air, bodies strewn across the debris and the streets, vehicles bursting into flames with the neighbouring shops and offices reduced to rubble. In total 168 lives were lost, including 33 children. Countless people were injured with local hospitals overflowing in a similar way as they have been during Covid and now in the Ukraine war.

My own personal memories of the final stages of the war are somewhat blurred. After the nail-biting weeks following the D-Day landings, the Allied invasions of western France were eventually successful. There were setbacks, not least the unsuccessful Battle of Arnhem, Holland in September 1944. Soon after this, Mary became friends with a delightful young man who, as a parachutist at Arnhem, suffered severe shell shock from which, we envisaged, he was unlikely to recover.

In desperation, towards the end of the year, Germany gathered together reserve forces to launch a massive counter-offensive in the Ardennes, but this collapsed early in 1945. The aim of the allies was a rigorous advance on Berlin from all fronts. The Russians were already making great headway in their advance from the east and the American, French and British forces each played their strategic roles from the west in order to bring about the capture of Berlin. Germany put up a fierce defence, but rapidly lost territory, ran out of supplies and exhausted its options. With the eventual capture of Berlin by the Russians in late April, the war was virtually over. On 30 April Hitler committed suicide in his bunker. Germany's final, unconditional surrender came on 7 May. The following day, Tuesday, 8 May 1945, was declared Victory in Europe Day (VE Day) marking the formal end of the European war. Street parties took place in towns and villages up and down the country, including one in Walton Road in Sidcup where we lived. All down the Mall and outside Buckingham Palace there were never-to-be-forgotten scenes of jubilation. We have seen similar scenes more recently when these same Spitfires took to the skies as part of the Platinum Jubilee celebrations of Queen Elizabeth II in 2022 and again at King Charles' coronation one year later.

We may have celebrated VE Day but it wasn't until the August, following the dropping by the Americans of two atomic bombs on Hiroshima and Nagasaki, with the loss of hundreds of thousands of civilians, that the war against Japan ended (VJ Day), marking the end of World War II, one of the deadliest and most destructive wars in history. When President Harry S Truman announced on 15 August 1945 that Japan had surrendered unconditionally, war-weary citizens around the world erupted in celebration.

Now that WW2 had ended, the Allies in Europe were faced with occupying the land they had conquered, incorporating the many heavily destroyed cities. Germany was divided into zones and occupied by the British, Americans, Russians and French respectively with the city of Berlin divided similarly into sectors.

Never in my wildest dreams would I have envisaged then that only nine years later I would be living there and experiencing its aftermath for myself.

Epilogue

During this latter period of the war and the months and years beyond, I owe an enormous amount to the Girl Guide movement. I had enrolled as a Brownie whilst living as an evacuee in Chesham. Then in 1942, not long after we had returned home, I joined a local Guide company where Mary was already a patrol leader.

We would meet in a church hall on Friday evenings—a five-minute cycle ride from home. Mother never mollycoddled me and she seemed to have little problem with me cycling around on my own. If a siren sounded to let us know that an air raid was imminent, following my mother's instructions, wherever I was, I would either cycle quickly to the nearest air raid shelter or return home. I don't think I was unduly frightened at the time.

I remember our Guide company as highly organised compared with others I came across. One couldn't just drift casually into a meeting as and when one pleased! To become a member, a solemn Guide promise was made in a special ceremony which took place in front of the other members of the company. There were three parts to the promise: duty to God, duty to King and Country and the keeping of the Guide Law. I took all this very seriously.

We had uniform inspection at most meetings. I was teased by Mary for taking greater care of my Guide uniform than I ever did of my school uniform! My Guide uniform was always carefully ironed and my tie properly knotted and tied.

At the enrolment ceremony we were given the trefoil badge. Its three leaves represented the threefold promise we had made. As enrolled Guides we were encouraged to shake with our left hand as a symbol of friendship. The Guide's aim to do a daily good turn is well known and that aim became part of my everyday living. Friday nights were to become the highlight of my week.

Looking back now on that latter part of the war, I see just a snippet of a turning point in my persona. I seemed to have developed something of a purpose in life and I was beginning to form meaningful friendships. Previously, although on the whole I enjoyed life, I was hampered by extreme shyness which I could not hide from others since it showed itself in my uncontrollable blushing. My self-esteem had been low and I had difficulty in making personal friends. I recall how good Mary's friends were to me; I was often invited with her to join them for family meals.

As a Guide I felt included and valued. I gradually gained badges in a variety of skills, all of which I wore proudly on the sleeves of my uniform. When I was given a promotion to captain my patrol I was over the moon and could scarcely believe it! My low self-esteem needed boosting!

Our Guide company and our brother Boy Scout company were affiliated to the United Reformed Church. Once a month we would assemble in the church porch, where we would prepare ourselves to attend the Sunday morning parade service. I was somewhat apprehensive when delegated to hold a banner and head the parade into the church and up the aisle, handing it over to a church official. It was not quite my forté but I did manage it!

I owe so much to my Guiding days at the end of the war. They gave me, in my teenage years, a purpose in my life that I subconsciously craved and, without fully knowing its significance at the time, I benefited from the Christian ethos to which I was exposed. God was less remote and more of a reality in my life.

And the hand of the Lord was with them
and a large number who believed turned
to the Lord. (Acts 11 v 21)

CHAPTER 5

Post-war,
1945–1954

When peace was declared in Europe in May 1945, I had lived over a third of my life during years of war. Emerging as a young adolescent, I scarcely knew what it was like to live in a country at peace. It was difficult to grasp fully that we were no longer in danger and had nothing to fear. Our freedom had been given back to us but at great cost. In Sidcup many bombed sites were daily reminders of this. There were flattened spaces where houses once stood and many other buildings were propped up, needing repair and restoration. We were fortunate that our house had not received a direct hit but there were problems with its foundations and we had to wait patiently in the queue for the repair of ceilings and replacement windows. We were still subject to many restrictions with ongoing food shortages. Rationing of certain foods, as well as clothes, didn't completely end until 1954. So, it certainly wasn't a bed of roses in that next stage following the war, as I had naively anticipated.

Although still living at home, Mary had begun her training at Regent Street Polytechnic in London as a chiropodist.

A social life was opening up for her. Mother was engrossed and valuing her full-time secretarial work in the City. Father continued to be completely focused and committed to his journalism, enjoying every minute of it. Mother complained that he was seriously underpaid and should be asking for a rise in his salary. Yet for him, now freed from his warden duties on the *Kentish Times* roof top, the end of the war meant he could focus on reporting—the job he loved.

In the autumn of 1945, I left Chislehurst Grammar School to continue my education at Blackheath High School in Blackheath Village just eight miles from our home in Sidcup. Mother was not happy with the way I was beginning to develop a 'lazy' English accent, reaching the conclusion that this was the consequence of the Education Act of 1944. This radical act aimed to remove the inequalities which remained in the post-war secondary education system in Britain. For example, up to that time my parents were required to pay fees for us at our grammar school. I am sad to say that Mother was quite class conscious at that time and I recall that she classified herself as 'lower middle class'.

My new school was founded in 1880 and was part of the Girls' Public Day School Trust. The senior department was housed in a purpose-built Victorian building in Wemys Road in the centre of the village, a stone's throw from the station and bus stops.

At last, I was in the right class for my age! I was relatively happy in my new school, enjoying the work as well as some of the extra-curricular activities offered, such as ballroom dancing and individual piano lessons. I enjoyed the piano and took a number of Royal College of Music exams.

School lessons took place in the mornings from 8.30—1.30. After lunch, three of the afternoons were allocated to sport and the other two afternoons we were free to go home, or if we wished we could do our 'prep' in school. As I wasn't that keen on sport and quite independent for my age, I would often sneak off on my bike after lunch and make for home! Nobody seemed to notice my absence. The ride would take just over an hour, and provided the weather was favourable, I much preferred it to the journey via Lee Green by bus and train.

I thrived then, as now, on encouragement and that is what my father provided for me, especially in the area of education. It meant so much to me when he would put down his tools and come along to open evenings, speech days, or a school play or concert.

Due to my disrupted education over the war years, I never really reached my potential. My exam results were mediocre, but fortunately high enough that a number of careers were open to me. I had been appointed as a deputy head girl for my last few months at the school and that looked good on my CV!

The headmistress allowed me to delay leaving school until I had decided on a career that I felt would suit me. I had to bear in mind that my parents' finances were such that any further education would need to be restricted to just two years of training. At that time most girls were taking up careers either in the medical world or in teaching.

After some deliberation I decided to take up a career in pharmacy, starting with a 20-month paid apprenticeship in a pharmacy attached to a Boots retail shop in nearby Orpington, followed by a two-year training programme in Nottingham. After just six months of training, I came to a wise and realistic conclusion that pharmacy was not for me. I didn't relish the thought of being cooped up in a dispensary day after day. I saw it as a demanding yet dull job; accuracy and precision were of the essence, neither of which were my forté! I came to realise that I was a 'people person', which meant a career that would give me face-to-face contact with people.

I had dabbled a bit with teaching, partly through the Guide movement and also in a Sunday school. I wondered whether teaching might be a more suitable career for me.

After my short-lived pharmacy training, I knew that a future career choice was not to be taken lightly. If a teaching career was now on the agenda, I wanted a trial run first. I didn't want to make another mistake. In today's world the culture is so different; we see folk exercising greater flexibility, freely changing careers at different stages of their lives.

With confidence and determination, I approached the local education department where I was welcomed with open arms to serve for five months as an unqualified teaching assistant in a local village school at Foots Cray, close to where we lived. I was over the moon. At that time the school was oversubscribed due to an influx of Gypsy children of indeterminate age. In order to cope with the increased numbers, two classes were accommodated in one room by means of a halfway back-to-back division. My section of the room was the reception class, which included a few Gypsy children. This proved to be an experience not to be forgotten and a challenge that I enjoyed.

The classroom was heated by a stove. Every morning individual bottles of milk (1/3 pint) were warmed beside this stove and given to each child to be consumed at the morning break. As milk was still rationed, the state supplied these small bottles of milk to every youngster in primary schools to ensure they were adequately nourished.

The headmistress came across as something of a tyrant. I thought her sadistic in the way she treated the pupils when they misbehaved. They had to stand in front of the whole school and be caned across their hands or backsides; screams would be heard. We must be thankful for today's legislation that prohibits corporal punishment.

Although I loved the youngsters and enjoyed teaching them, I was relieved to be asked to move on at the end of term to another village school in St Mary Cray nearby. The building was old. The toilet blocks used by staff and children alike were outside in the playground. I recall trying to last all day until lessons were over and the children gone! I thoroughly enjoyed the ethos of the school and my experience there. I was paid very little but I was pleased with what I did receive. I received two good references and knew without a doubt that teaching was for me!

I continued as a member of the Guide movement. There was a memorable occasion soon after the end of the war when a few Guides from our company were invited to attend a thanksgiving service in Canterbury Cathedral taken by the Archbishop, Geoffrey Fisher. In the bombing in June 1942 the Cathedral had been a key target. Four men who had been designated as 'fire watchers' rushed to the roof of the Cathedral when the first incendiary bomb struck. Their job was to spot and put out incendiary bombs before they could cause a fire. Thanks to their bravery the Cathedral survived serious fires, although greater damage was caused later by high explosives.

When the thanksgiving service was held some months after the end of the war, the roof had been covered and was no longer open to the elements. The damage we saw all around us in no way deterred us. With the Cathedral packed to overflowing, it was a moving and emotional service. I was thrilled to have been selected to be part of it. Looking so proud and smart in our uniforms, we sang hymns of thanksgiving from our hearts with great gusto; no doubt we could be heard way beyond the Cathedral walls! Prayers of thanksgiving, led by the Archbishop and others, were so meaningful as it fully dawned on us that the Lord had brought us safely through the war and we were at peace.

On 3 September 1949 (exactly 10 years after the beginning of the war), I left England to spend a never-to-be-forgotten fortnight's holiday in the Bernese Oberland of Switzerland, returning just a couple of days before the start of my teacher training in Cheltenham.

In order to pay for the trip, I worked most of the summer in a private business restaurant in the Strand in London. Working in a restaurant was not really 'up my street' but I survived and it was well worth it as it enabled me to pay my way on the holiday independently of my parents.

We were a travelling party of 20, all of similar age, with a slightly older married couple as our leaders. What we experienced on that holiday was in sharp contrast to the austerity of life back home. Switzerland had remained neutral throughout the war, serving as a safe haven for refugees and others escaping the atrocities of war.

We met at Waterloo Station to board a train for the first leg of the journey to the ferry at Folkestone, which then took us across the Channel to Boulogne. We travelled overnight by train to Geneva, where we changed onto another train which took us to the lakeside town of Spiez in the German speaking region of Switzerland. The mountain scenery on that train was spectacular; I was overwhelmed by its grandeur and beauty. Kandersteg, our ultimate destination, sat high above the Spiezersee. It was a characterful Alpine village approached by bus. The entire journey was marked by precision, for which the country is renowned.

My clear memory of our stay at our hotel was the luxury and richness of its food. I had never known or eaten food like it! Cream galore! The packed lunches we were given for our daily outings were like no other!

We purchased special travel passes, which gave us reductions on boat trips, mountain railways and chair lifts. There was one particular episode I recall when I inadvertently dropped my travel pass into the lake at Interlaken as I was clambering off a ferry! There was concern and consternation all round and I was both angry and embarrassed by my carelessness. My pass was miraculously retrieved by one of the crew and survived for further use!

At that stage in my life, I could have wished for nothing better than all that this wonderful holiday provided: stunning scenery that I had only seen in books, sumptuous foods, so much of which I had never savoured before, excursions by bus, boat, mountain railways and chair lifts and the special Sunday services we were able to attend, taken by a British chaplain who was himself enjoying a busman's holiday. I take my hat off to the friends who organised this trip.

We returned home with just time enough to pack and send my trunk on in advance to St Mary's College in Cheltenham. During those post-war years teacher training was two years instead of three but we made up the time with shorter vacations and longer college hours. My employment as an unqualified teacher in those two village primary schools gave me the confidence I needed as I started at Cheltenham. I even felt a few steps ahead of the other students. I have never regretted my decision to teach. It was, without a doubt, my vocation.

St Mary's College ranked amongst the three best teacher training colleges in the country. I chose divinity as my main subject with theory of music as my subsidiary. Divinity was an unfortunate choice, as I did not warm to the syllabus nor to the lecturer. She persistently tried to thwart those of us, and me in particular, whose faith was strong, genuine and biblically based on the authority of the scriptures.

Teaching practice was central to our curriculum. We were allocated schools scattered around the local area, as well as places further afield like Bristol, which was an hour away by bus. My last main teaching practice was a month at a primary school in Gloucester. I chose a special project for my class of 30 nine-year-olds: the creation and functioning of our own post office. It went down a treat! The youngsters and I put our 'all' into it. To crown it all, I gained an overall A* grade with distinction for my teaching, which compensated for my somewhat mediocre academic grades.

My newly found Christian faith, which I have written about in the epilogue at the end of this chapter, took me into unexpected new pastures. I became college 'rep' for chapel services, which were held at St Paul's, our brother college a couple of miles away. I was also appointed president of our own thriving and well-attended Christian Union. As both roles involved organisation I was in my element: planning meetings, inviting outside speakers to 'open' meetings, including two or three well-known speakers from Oxford Inter-Collegiate Christian Union (OICCU). These were well attended by those interested in exploring the Christian faith, even when they claimed they had little or no faith at all.

My original plans to be confirmed through my church in Sidcup had been thwarted due to the obligatory confirmation classes clashing with the timings of a Bible class to which I was committed outside the church. Arrangements were subsequently made for me to be confirmed in Gloucester Cathedral, which I saw as quite an honour. Madeline Wheen, who played such an integral and strategic role in my journey of faith, travelled from Chislehurst to Gloucester to attend the service. I much appreciated and valued this thoughtful and kind gesture. My father was there as well.

Other special occasions included a talk I was asked to give at an open meeting at Birmingham University. All this sounds awesome to me now but I took it in my stride at the time. Public teaching didn't faze me.

I always looked forward to Saturdays when, regular as clockwork, I would receive a newsy letter from my father. In it, unknown to my mother, a pocket money 'top-up' of seven shillings and sixpence would be enclosed. This gesture meant a lot to me. I would eagerly read his letter, written in impeccable English but almost illegible handwriting. What I enjoyed most were his termly trips to visit me at the college; Mother and Mary would visit too, often staying overnight.

I made special lasting friendships at Cheltenham. I am still in contact with one, Hazel Duffin, née Sanders, who now lives in Devon. My maiden surname was also Saunders and Hazel and I first met in an alphabetical queue for the distribution of books at the start of our first term. We haven't met for a few years but we phone one another once or twice a week and enjoy our catch-up chats. It was she who reminded me of the actual amount of my father's monetary weekly gift, as well as the 'clash' I had with my divinity lecturer.

All good things come to an end and in the summer of 1951, I was back living with my parents in Shoreham, Kent embarking on the first of three years as a qualified teacher in a church primary school in Bromley, Kent. Due to the war, there was a dearth of teachers, so newly qualified teachers could be selective in their choice of school. At that time, salaries were higher in schools in outer London. With that in mind, as well as the quality of the school and its staff, I was drawn to the post.

I remember so well the two very special national celebrations that coincided on 2 June 1953; the first was the queen's coronation taking place in Westminster Abbey and the second was the news that Edmund *Hillary* of New Zealand and Tenzin Norgay, a Sherpa of Nepal, had become the first explorers to reach and conquer the highest point of earth— the 29,035ft summit of Mount *Everest*. It may have been a wet and dismal day in London as thousands of us watched the queen's procession, but hearts were full of joy and pride so evident in the happy faces and shouts of jubilation.

Epilogue

When I became a leader within the Guide movement, I and others would regularly meet on Chislehurst Common to enjoy a variety of activities. Daylight and weather permitting we would end our time together with a singsong around a campfire. I loved the 'togetherness' that these campfires created. Familiar Guide songs were sung lustily. Before we went our separate ways, we would have a short epilogue of a 'thought for the day' and a closing prayer, normally led by our Guide commissioner, Madeline Wheen. I recall a memorable overnight hike in late November in sub-zero temperatures. It was, without doubt, a never-to-be-forgotten experience and challenge for us all!

On one particular summer's evening, Madeline shared with us her own personal Christian journey of faith and the way in which it had evolved and turned her life around. In previous epilogues I shared that, as a young child, I only had to look at nature and the night sky to believe in a Creator God. Subsequently, I began to believe that he was personally involved in our lives. He had so clearly answered the prayers of thousands following the Days of National Prayer during the war. I craved clarity and understanding of what, to me, seemed somewhat of a jigsaw. As a Girl Guide, I had made a solemn promise to serve God and King. This promise I didn't make lightly, but I was only too aware of my imperfections. I needed help from someone to whom I could be accountable.

Following the testimony, Madeline invited anyone who might be interested in exploring the Christian faith further to come to her home for a chat and informal discussion. I loved all that the Guides had offered me, particularly the leadership role which had given me the confidence I had lacked. However, I still suffered with shyness, particularly when relating to those in leadership roles. However, I was so determined to explore Christianity that I took the bull by the horns and asked if I could chat with her on my own.

A few days later on the dot of our agreed time, I left my cycle in her garden and, with trepidation, knocked on her front door; I was warmly greeted by Madeline and taken into her living room. I don't think I realised at the time that she would have been delighted to see and chat with ME! My low self-esteem has been a hindrance to me much of my life, leaving me feeling I was unwanted and making me somewhat apologetic for my very existence!

This visit was the start of a succession of others and I gradually began to feel a bit more relaxed as I sought for understanding and truth. With the Bible open acting as our reference, I was helped to understand and interpret the truths behind the stories of the prophets of the Old Testament and began to see these fulfilled in the life of Jesus, God's one and only true Son, who was both human and divine, which was a difficult concept for many to fathom. I began to understand that he was without sin and his life was a living example that I needed to follow. I realised that the sacrifices conducted by the high priests, which I had read about in the Old Testament, were no longer needed. Details of the atrocities inflicted within German concentration camps during the war were gradually emerging into the public domain and were much in my mind at that time. I now needed to accept that Jesus loved us so much that he died on the cross on behalf of all sinners, and forgiveness is available and free for us *all*, even for those responsible for the death of innocent victims in Belsen and Auschwitz, the sites of which I would visit later on in my life.

There was just one difficulty I finally needed to resolve, and that was belief in the resurrection. Madeline lent me the book *Who moved the stone?* by Frank Morison, a thoughtfully written book exploring the rationale and the truth of the resurrection accounts in the Gospels. I would recommend that book to anyone exploring the truths of Christianity.

Gradually things seemed to fall into place and the jigsaw came together. I began to realise that if the Bible IS true, then the Christian faith had implications for me. Madeline herself was a living example of a genuine practising believer. Only a couple of years later she became the first lady warden at Lee Abbey, a well-known conference and retreat centre in north Devon, and gave many years of fruitful service to its guests. I owe so much to her, without whom I might never have come to faith. It was a time of celebration for me but a tough road lay ahead.

I was put in touch with the vicar of Christ Church, an Anglican church in Sidcup, and I started to attend its services enjoying its worship and fellowship.

However, I did have one seemingly unavoidable setback during those early years as a practising Christian. My path crossed with those whose theology focused on abstention from worldly pleasure. It was a theology of negativity and legalism. By way of example, I was told that as a Christian I shouldn't attend the cinema, theatre, to meet in groups and not to partake in boy/girl relationships without a chaperone, not to drink alcohol etc. For practising Christians these were all considered 'no-go' areas.

My mind boggles now as to what one could or could not do on Sundays. I became entwined in this way of thinking, feeling obliged to abstain from what I had seen previously as innocent life pleasures.

So here I was with the joy of becoming a Christian, relishing my newly found relationship with God, as well as with fellow Christians, yet needing to navigate this adherence to a negative approach to life. So much discernment was needed. The timing of the start of college life was God-sent. Much of that legalism was shaken off there, only to come back later in my time in Germany where worldly pleasures were part of my everyday life. However, the truths of Christianity have never left me.

CHAPTER 6

Occupied Germany, 1954–1957

I wonder what it was in 1954 that prompted me to apply for a teaching post in a co-educational mixed comprehensive boarding school for the children of British Forces personnel in Occupied Germany? I did have a contact in the school through my mother, otherwise I would probably never have known of the school's existence. The fact that it was located in the lake district area of Schleswig Holstein near Lübeck was an attraction for me. Marjorie Schofield, a former colleague of my mother in the City of London, had recently joined her husband Mike who had been appointed to be head of the art department at the school. Marjorie and I had met on a few occasions and I became aware of my itchy feet to leave my home nest. I was thrilled when I was invited to visit them over the Easter holidays of 1954. They lived in a large apartment and had plenty of room for me. I needed a holiday and it gave me the opportunity to see if I liked the school, and should a suitable vacancy occur, apply for it. Despite my enthusiasm, I didn't want to make a mistake as I had done with pharmacy.

The time was ripe. Mary had already left the nest, having married two years previously. If I did not do something about moving away from home soon, I could find myself living in my parents' home ad infinitum—not an exciting prospect for someone born with an adventurous spirit. Teaching in another part of the UK would not earn enough for me to be able to live independently. My sights were now focused on teaching abroad in a British Forces school, perhaps in Malta or British Occupied Germany or even Singapore. Why not Germany?

At the start of the Easter holidays, I was off like a shot wanting to make the most of my three-week holiday. My car was too old to drive on the Continent so I travelled by train. I decided I would break the journey to visit the small market town of Hameln, renowned for its association with the legend of the Pied Piper. I was enamoured with it at first sight, as much as with a handsome young man from Lancashire who I met there working at the NAAFI. He showed me around the town and a friendship began to develop. That summer he even visited me in my home in Kent, but it wasn't long before I knew the relationship wasn't for me and it fizzled out quite naturally. A flash in the pan and quickly forgotten!

The next part of the journey was in a cramped and overcrowded compartment travelling through the night. It was not a pleasant experience. After three changes of trains, it was a relief to arrive at Plön station just a mile or so from the school. The pupils were away at the time enjoying their Easter holiday.

The school buildings, scattered across acres of attractive grounds, were just amazing, as was the lakeside location and the range of sports amenities. Marjorie and Mike looked after me well. I even went on a popular half day five-lake sail.

What I gleaned through that visit was exciting. The school certainly ticked all the boxes for me. But (and it was a big 'but') I was only just approaching my twenty-third birthday and my lack of secondary school experience could well prove a barrier should a teaching place become available.

Soon after I returned home a post for a maths and general subjects' teacher was advertised in the *Times Educational Supplement*. I sent my application off to the War Office and was subsequently invited for interview.

How I ever survived the interview I shall never know. I recall the formidable interview board (ten men and one woman) sitting in a long row in front of me, firing questions at me right, left and centre to test my suitability.

To my surprise I was offered the post! Just four months later, having passed my medical and signed the Official Secrets Act, Mary's husband, Hugh, kindly gave me a lift to Harwich Harbour to board an overnight service ferry on the seven-hour crossing to the Hook of Holland—the first leg of my journey.

I was delighted to be joined by a number of other teachers bound for King Alfred School, with a few like me who had just been appointed to the staff. I will never forget that crossing; it was not a good introduction to my new life.

I was appalled at the state of the service ferry and the conditions in the cabins. We had no option but to get on with it. The crossing was rough but, fortunately, I rarely suffer from sea sickness. Nonetheless, we were greatly relieved to see the docks of the Hook of Holland and stand on dry land!

An old service coach was waiting to take us on the seven-hour drive to Neumünster. I would guess that no repairs had been carried out on the Autobahns since the war; they were bumpy to say the least with a succession of long diversions when the road was unfit for purpose.

A dramatic turn for the better awaited us at Neumünster. We were welcomed by officers of the British Army as well as by a senior member of the teaching staff and were treated like royalty.

For the last leg of the journey, we were in the hands of a young and courteous German driver. We may have been exhausted from the long journey, but we cheered upon arrival as the barrier gate at the entrance to King Alfred School was lifted and we were given such a warm reception, which more than made up for it. A glass of wine and an appetising meal served by friendly and hospitable Germans brought us back to life!

The occupation of Germany following the war saw the country divided between zones under the jurisdiction of the Americans, Canadians, British, French and Russians respectively. The first four were in the western two-thirds of Germany, whilst the Soviet zone was in the eastern third. The Russian zone to the east was close to our school, separated from us by the Lübeck–Kiel canal. Its proximity made the school quite vulnerable. Defence needed to be in place in the event of any conflict during these early years of the Cold War and this was expensive to maintain.

In 1954 Germany was still reeling from the aftermath of the war. Most Germans longed to put the horrors of the past behind them and focus on the opportunities to start again. New beginnings were certainly needed. The massive bombing had taken its toll: the loss of so many lives had left thousands grieving loved ones, homes destroyed and lives shattered.

It was into that war-torn country that I started a new stage in life with my own lingering memories of the war. Germans, eager to start afresh, took on a variety of posts within the school, most of which, apart from teachers of German, were of an auxiliary nature. I was well aware that it was a testing time for both Germans and British to be working side by side. In the sight of God, we were all equals; pride of victory only went as far as the need to quench the evil activities of Nazism. I personally struggled with two or three Brits whose thinking, in my opinion, was not acceptable; some of them treated their German colleagues with an attitude of contempt. Despite my own experiences of war, I discovered I was not hampered by attitudes of class or nationality; I had no difficulty in accepting others just as they were.

There are two particular German colleagues who remain in my mind; they were such delightful individuals, contributing so positively to the general ethos of the school. One was our harbour master, who had worked tirelessly retrieving 26 boats from the lake and repairing two launches. He had overall responsibility for the King Alfred School Yacht Club. The other was Frau Herfurth who was much loved by us all as a colleague and teacher of German.

King Alfred School had been built before the war as a German naval training base. Following the war, the site was handed over to the British Forces Education Service (BFES) and was opened in 1948 as a co-educational mixed ability (comprehensive as it now known) boarding school, the first of its kind in Europe. It had an idyllic location by the Größer Plönersee, on the outskirts of the small market town of Plön, famous for its historic schloss. Sailing and swimming in the summer, skiing and skating in the winter, athletics in an Olympic-sized stadium, horse riding and a variety of traditional sports were all offered as part of the curriculum for the 600 pupils educated there. For some pupils their time at the school was short lived as their fathers might only be stationed in Germany for a couple of years. Other pupils, whose fathers held civilian posts, were able to stay for almost the whole span of their secondary education.

The school owed much to its first headmaster, Freddie Spencer Chapman, who had previously been a housemaster at Gordonstoun School. After his studies at Cambridge, and before turning to teaching, Chapman's adventurous spirit and love of the natural world took root, leading him to join expeditions to the Arctic and the Himalayas. He brought his wonderful visionary approach to creating and establishing an outstanding, unique and much valued school which was well ahead of its time, and on which his successor, Hugh Wallis Hoskin, appointed in 1953, was able to build.

As single staff we were given rooms for our first few nights in a block reserved normally for visitors. On that first evening, following a short rest after supper, we were invited to the deputy head's nearby apartment for a welcome 'after-dinner' drink. Living in style to say the least! I began to realise I was likely to be in for a good time in my new job!

It was late August with several days of holiday remaining before the pupils arrived and the term started. This gave us time to acclimatise to our surroundings and to settle into our apartments. Most teaching staff lived in one of the five residential houses (separate buildings scattered across the central compass of the grounds) named after well-known people: Churchill, Fleming, Nansen, Roosevelt and Temple. Each had its own housemaster and housemistress and two 'live-in' supporting staff. I was in Roosevelt for a couple of terms in that supporting role and then moved to Churchill House. Boys and girls of each house were in separate wings of the same building, separated by what was unofficially named, in Churchill, a 'chastity' door!

Early on that first morning we were given a tour of the school grounds and buildings and then shown the inside of Butler Hall, where all the pupils were served three good meals each day, as well as drinks and snacks mid-morning and at teatime before extra-curricular activities began. It was a vast room with capacity to seat and serve meals to

600 pupils at the same time. Germans were employed to work in the kitchens with a British person in overall charge.

Towards the periphery of the grounds and near where the original (but now bolted) entrance gate stood was St George's Chapel. Here a service, led by the padre, took place every Sunday morning which, once I had settled into the school routine, I always enjoyed attending. After the school closed down our school reunions would include a church service led by a former padre—these were always moving and much valued occasions. I was involved and invited from time to time to give a talk or lead the prayers.

Our school tour took in the 'quarter deck', which was considered the focal point of the school. In the centre of the quarter deck stood a flagpole and a bell. The Union Jack and King Alfred School flags were raised at the start of the day and lowered at dusk by our notorious and punctilious school porter. The flagpole and bell remain there to this day.

The 'quarter deck' was surrounded on three sides by buildings. On one side stood the school hospital and medical centre run by our resident British doctor, the headmaster's office, administrative offices and staff room. At right angles to that lay the teaching block. As I looked into the classrooms, I was struck by the responsibilities of teaching secondary school youngsters that lay ahead of me. I remember being excited at the prospect of taking up the reins of teaching some of the same subjects I had taught back home (namely maths, English and geography) but to a higher level and to an older age group.

At right angles to the teaching block were the apartments for some of the single staff as well as visitors to the school—friends and relatives and others who could be quite prestigious!

All personnel would enter and leave the school through a nearby security gate with its security guard on duty 24/7; in the same proximity stood a primary school building where the younger children of staff members were taught.

Close to the teaching block was a small, artistically shaped pond; its attractive Monet-style arched bridge had been formally opened by the Norwegians shortly before my arrival. After daily morning assemblies in Butler Hall, pupils and staff alike would informally file across this lovely bridge to the classroom block.

Our staff had its own officers' mess, located on the periphery of the grounds, close to the headmaster's residence. Here we were served breakfast, lunch and our evening meal; afternoon tea was available in the lounge there if needs be! The chefs and those who waited on us were German nationals; they were of a friendly and courteous disposition, but sadly a very small minority did not treat them with the respect they deserved. The standard and service offered surpassed that of any first-class hotel, which was remarkable only nine years after the end of the war. As I reflected on the war and the many wasted lives, I needed to pinch myself from time to time in order to believe the awful events of war had happened in my own childhood, only a decade previously.

At first, I had to adjust to a lifestyle totally alien to the one I had been used to. I certainly relished the prospect of having most of my practical needs met in style! I loved the cooked breakfasts with so much choice—something not the norm now! Tolerance is not one of my virtues and I certainly wasn't all that tolerant to chatterboxes at the breakfast table. Fortunately, we had British newspapers delivered daily to the mess (a day late), behind which I could hide. I had a 'bat-woman' who cleaned my room and made the bed on a daily basis. Now, at 90 years old, I would relish this luxury! I don't enjoy household chores and I just loved being completely spoilt. With no washing up to do and clothes miraculously disappearing into the laundry and reappearing the next day, neatly ironed and folded, it was a luxury lifestyle to which I never had the privilege to return.

However, the luxury of being waited on did compensate for the hard work expected of us during term time; with lessons on Saturday mornings, we were given one afternoon off a week and a weekend free once a month.

We adhered to a marathon of rotas. In our respective houses, the day started with the person on house duty, ensuring that pupils were up in good time to wash, dress and then make their way to the dining hall a few minutes' walk away. Here they were under the supervision of Jack Stirk, who was responsible not just for the order and discipline of the pupils but also for the provision of meals and the kitchen staff. This was no easy task, but he was strict and did it well. When behaviour in the dining hall was not acceptable teaching staff would be called to exercise their authority.

Following school policy, staff were responsible for supervising pupils throughout the day. After breakfast, the pupils returned to their boarding houses to make their beds and tidy their dormitory, ready for the daily inspection. This was also when some pupils would be seen rushing to finish 'prep' left from the previous evening. Then it was off to the daily school assembly, led by the headmaster or his deputy. Attendance at assembly was obligatory for teaching staff; this went against the grain for many and there were sneaky absences! Then staff and pupils would troop over the bridge to the teaching block for lessons in the academic subjects. Practical subjects such as chemistry, cookery and woodwork took place in their own specially equipped and designated rooms. At the sound of the first bell from the 'quarter deck' and then a second bell five minutes later, lessons began. The mid-morning break of half an hour was much valued by pupils and staff alike; staff spent this precious half hour in our nearby staff room. Following morning lessons and after lunch, there was a compulsory and supervised rest period for the pupils before the start of afternoon lessons.

Activities in summer took place in the evenings with the pupils enjoying a variety of sports, including water sports and sailing. For those who had joined the Combined Cadet Force (CCF) and Scout, Guide and Sea Ranger movements there were regular meetings. What amazing opportunities our pupils had! In the winter months lessons took place in the evenings, enabling activities to be enjoyed in the daylight. The winters were harsh, especially between January and late March. With the car I had bought laid up for fear of accidents on ungritted skiddy roads and the sub-zero temperatures,

I didn't enjoy the spring term, as it was called. The youngsters, however, revelled in skiing and skating. I was on a rota to supervise these activities but when temperatures were particularly low and I was so cold, there were times when I managed to wriggle out of them!

After the evening meal those on duty had to return to their houses. In my house there was a renowned time of fond 'goodnights' taking place in our quad just outside the main entrance, between pupils who had developed boy/girl friendships within the same house. Homework in the common room was followed by leisure time before bedtime. These were staggered and according to age with the school prefects given more freedom as to when to go to bed.

So, when were staff meetings fitted in to this daily tight schedule? It was essential and, dare I say, obligatory that we all attended these. Important notices were given out during the morning breaks, but the longer ones took place at 10pm when the pupils were in bed and under the supervision of their house matron and senior prefects.

Within the premises of the school, we had our own shop open at specific hours six days a week. Our internal BAOR (British Army of the Rhine) currency was used for internal transactions within the school, with a fixed exchange rate. These were called BAFs (British Armed Force), which we bought with Deutsch marks. Our German bank accounts ran alongside our British bank accounts, into which our salaries were paid. As the exchange rate was in our favour, we would make the most of this well-supplied shop. BAFs were used to buy many other commodities and services within our precincts, such as the hairdresser, our afternoon tea at the cricket pavilion on Sunday afternoons.

We worked hard and certainly deserved and eagerly awaited the weekday half day off we had each week woven into our timetables. On our half days, as soon as morning lessons were over, the single folk on the teaching staff would hop into waiting taxis to take us for our planned outings. I often chose to go further afield to Lübeck or Neumünster for the traditional 'Kaffee and Küchen'. Austerity seemed to have gone out of the window as Kuchen were in plentiful supply surpassing anything I had ever seen back in the UK where cake was limited to doughnuts, Swiss rolls and jam tarts! The gift shops were enormously tempting; we rarely returned empty handed. I tended to allocate free Saturday afternoons for a visit to our local town of Plön. There was the schloss to see and plenty of individual shops eager to sell us their wares.

When I happened to be free on Sundays and eager for a jaunt somewhere different and further afield, I and a friend would drive to Denmark for lunch. Often it would be Flensburg but with an early start Søndetborg was possible. To sample Danish food was a treat, and trips such as these made such a difference and were a genuine bonus to my life then.

I recall another trip when two or three of us took a school taxi to the sands near Travemünde where we had the amazing experience of walking on the frozen Baltic Sea.

I loved going of an evening to Neumünster and Lübeck where a number of classical orchestral concerts took place which were very popular.

Photography had always been of special interest to me. With the guidance of Mary, I even learned and was proud to develop my own films. The camera I bought in Plön became a precious possession for many years.

Towards the end of my first year at the school I surprised the staff when I appeared one day driving a Morris Minor car—the first lady of the school to buy a new one! I was the envy of some and teased by others, who said the only reason I could afford to buy it was because I refrained from drinking too many pink gins in the evenings at the bar! Cars were free of import duty for British personnel so were relatively cheap to buy. I think mine was around £300!

There was much excitement amongst the pupils towards the end of term, especially at Christmas. Cases began to be packed several days before the end of term. Then on the day of departure they were taken down in school lorries to Plön railway station.

The pupils had their own special train to take them to their destination close to where their fathers were stationed. These were scattered across the British zone of Germany and it would take several hours for the train to complete its mission. The staff would congregate on the platform for what was always an emotional send-off, with heads hanging out of windows and hands waving as the train started to chug out of the station and disappear from sight. We too were waving our 'au revoir' from the platform, feeling quite desolate when it was all over. As I write now, I realise how fond we must have been of the youngsters. They were with us 24/7 and were so much part of our lives and the focus of all we were doing. Little would I have believed then that, nearly 70 years later, I would be still seeing them, most in their retirement years at our annual London Wyvern reunions.

Some of us would be there to greet them when they returned at the start of the new term. We needed to look out for any, amongst those joining us for the first time, who might quietly be suffering from homesickness. Understanding and empathy were needed, and an awareness that boys were more prone to homesickness than girls but more likely to hide it. Most housemasters were not naturally as empathetic as their female counterparts so I fear the more introverted boys lost out.

One boy actually ran away shortly after he arrived, causing great consternation to all. With guards on duty day and night at the school barrier leading into the road, escape that way was almost impossible, so he must have headed through the unfamiliar open woods, fields and undergrowth surrounding the school grounds. His disappearance had to be reported to the military authorities. Knowing this was a serious incident, they took quick action and found our boy within a few hours of being reported missing. What a relief for the parents, who had obviously been informed and travelled up so they could comfort and reassure him. As I look back, we did have quite a responsibility in caring and protecting these young lives in what was still quite a vulnerable country full of unknowns. However, the general ethos of the school was a very happy one with so much going on to counteract homesickness.

Our holidays started a couple of days later than those of the pupils and ended a few days before they returned. Married staff who had comfortable and homely apartments would often stay on, taking their main holiday once or twice a year. For those of us who were single it was a different kettle of fish. Some would take advantage of the two annual free rail passes allotted to us each year. These gave us the opportunity to take off to the southern German border crossings. Austria, Switzerland and Italy were among my favourites, but I did once meet up with two friends in Trieste on the border of Italy and Yugoslavia, from which we took a train to Athens in southern Greece. That last leg of the journey was unhygienic to say the least and we were herded like cattle. It was my worst travel experience, and thankfully never to be repeated!

Each Christmas I would travel back to my home in the UK either by car or by train, crossing the Channel from Dunkerque where cars were lifted onto the ferry by crane. It was lovely and special on these occasions to be back again with the family. Mary and Hugh already had a son, Ian, born in 1954.

Two years later, whilst still working in Germany, I went on holiday to Italy. I was in Florence when Peter, my second nephew, arrived, the news of which was communicated to me by telegram sent to the post office by poste restante—a popular means of communication in those days.

Berlin, the former capital of Germany, had been divided into four zones of occupation, under the control of the United States, Britain, France and the Soviet Union respectively. At the hands of the Brits during the war, the city had suffered unbelievable bombing which had caused widespread devastation. It seems somewhat uncanny that I was drawn to the city. All I could do was accept and digest what I saw and understand that if this hadn't happened, we could have lost the war. I wanted to pass on words of encouragement to those who were living and working there so I did so in my faltering German to people who crossed my path during my three short stays there. I wanted to convey my understanding and empathy.

Following the war many years were spent clearing the millions of tonnes of rubble before building could start. I gather that men had been in short supply, having either moved away from the city or having sadly lost their lives. Women, many of whom had been Nazi supporters, were summoned by the authorities in their thousands to this British sector of Berlin where they resided, to take over the vital work of clearing the rubble, often working late into the night. They were supplied with a minimum allowance of food and drinks and were paid for their labours, but in some cases they received a pittance.

I recall my first visit on a free long weekend in 1955, travelling by train from a station close to Hannover en route to Berlin. We were locked securely into a cold and draughty compartment for several hours as we travelled slowly, stopping frequently through the Russian zone.

Two subsequent visits were by car. We drove through the Russian occupied zone from a designated checkpoint near Hannover along an autobahn, bumping over unavoidable potholes. As foreigners, we were banned from taking any diversion, let alone an exit. Legally, we were instructed to take no less than two and half hours and no more than four hours for our journey. If that rule was breached, I assume there would be trouble ahead!

I saw little rubble in the city—just large expanses of flattened areas, but with some positive signs of re-building. It was a devastating sight, particularly so as much of the bombing had been caused by the British Royal Air Force. The city remained divided into sectors. At that time there was no Berlin Wall. That wasn't erected until 1961 when the Iron Curtain of the Cold War split Berlin in two. In 1949 Bonn became the capital of Western Germany and remained so for 41 years, standing alongside London, Paris and Washington in the Cold War.

On my visits I was aware that East Berliners were forbidden to enter the Western zones. Western tourists were allowed across into East Berlin but were escorted on foot.

The famous and massive Brandenburg Gate, although damaged, was still standing there in isolation, reflecting the desolation of a ruined and unrecognisable former great capital. I found our short walking tour both moving and deeply depressing. We saw the entrance to Hitler's bunker. It was here he married Eva Braun shortly before they committed suicide together. Now it is part of a residential car park—forgotten and never to be earmarked for notoriety.

In the eastern zone, there were acres of ruins all around with little sign of much clearance or reconstruction. People living there looked so sad and wan. I don't regret the experience of visiting East Germany but it left with me a feeling of guilt and with ongoing thoughts of the futility of war. When I visited Hamburg soon after my arrival in the school, I was devastated to see it completely flat but with little sign of rebuilding.

It is gratifying to know that now both these cities are thriving and Berlin, once again holding its status as the capital of the reunified Germany, is restored and stunningly rebuilt. These short holidays gave me glimpses into the aftermath of the war both in Germany itself as well as in other countries, such as Italy, that I was able to visit.

Back in Plön there was never a dull moment for us teachers. We did all we could to bring out the best in all the pupils under our care. Metal work, woodwork, cookery, needlework, printing, farming and gardening formed part of the curriculum alongside a wealth of academic subjects. Each pupil was able to devote his or her time according to where their skills and interests lay, each encouraged to study for and sit the most appropriate public exam for them. Some left after O-levels to continue their education in the UK, whilst others continued in the sixth form to study and sit their A-levels. Some decided to leave school altogether and start work often using the practical skills they had been taught. One only has to pick up a copy of the school magazine, *The Red Dragon,* to see the wide range of subjects taught as well as the plethora of captivating activities offered. There was an abundance of specialist teachers who sailed proudly, dare I say, from building to building with their gowns billowing behind them! We even had a team competing in the finals of the *Top of the Form* broadcast on the radio.

Annual speech days were memorable occasions attended by dignitaries from across the British zone of Germany and beyond.

The school may have been run akin to Gordonstoun, but it offered so much to equip the pupils, with their wide spectrum of abilities and gifts, for their future lives and careers. For instance, I wonder how many schools at that time were able to enjoy their own radio programmes over the school's tannoy?

I have in my hand the 1957 summer term's *Red Dragon* magazine, which gives an insight into the activities and life of the school. It records the production of *HMS Pinafore,* performed by Churchill House with almost all 60 boys and 60 girls, as well as Churchill staff, playing their part. This production kept us frantically busy throughout that summer term, leading up to its three performances. The last, on our school speech day, was attended by a number of dignitaries. The performances were lauded by the audiences and it was certainly worth all the hard work, with the pleasure they gave.

Our house had previously produced and performed *The Gondoliers.* There were many other similar productions including a school production of *Tobias and the Angel* in the autumn of 1956. To quote from the *Red Dragon*: 'There can be no doubt that whatever the school tackles, we can be assured of excellent entertainment and a high standard of performance in every sphere, and we look forward with eagerness to the next production.'

Apart from teaching and those many duties of supervision, what part did I play in all of this? In some ways I see myself as 'small fry'—a cog in a large wheel making my own personal contribution to its life. Thanks to all I had learned in the Guide movement back in the UK, I was appointed captain of the Guide company at King Alfred School.

I loved teaching; it was a gift that gave me fulfilment and satisfaction. I also loved the opportunity to learn to sail, play the occasional game of tennis or badminton and saunter down to the cricket pavilion on a Sunday afternoon to enjoy the cricket and the afternoon tea provided. A bit like Lord's! On occasion, I even sneaked into a boxing match!

In all I have described, remember that King Alfred's was neither a grammar school nor a public school, but one of the first comprehensives in the world, offering education to a cross-section of abilities. To me there was little discrimination between pupils whose fathers were lance sergeants or lieutenant colonels, or whether they were from the army, RAF or civilian backgrounds. All learned and worked together as equals. Perhaps I could have played a greater part in encouraging relationships between the Germans and Brits as we worked together for the good of the next generation.

It is no wonder that the reunions, both at the school and annually in London, have proved so popular with around 100 attending. Starting in 1988 and in each of the next three decades we have had special celebratory occasions for the opening of the school staying in nearby Lübeck, but with many of the celebratory events taking place in the school itself.

Now that I had changed my career from teaching to the travel business, I was considered the appropriate person to organise the reunion. This included the reservation of flights, transfers and hotel. I was and still am in my element when organising travel groups so I readily agreed. I will never forget the celebration in 1998 when I took an oak tree from Sevenoaks on the flight. We planted the tree ceremoniously in the grounds of our former school which, since the school's closure, has been taken over once again by the German navy. We have been so grateful to those in authority there for their welcome to us over the years. I am glad to report the oak tree is still flourishing!

Each of the staff was on a renewable three-year contract. I was offered an extension but decided to call it a day. I knew that it had been a real privilege and experience to have been part of such an amazing school within the British Forces Education Service in Occupied Germany so soon after the war. I had learned so much about what it was like to live and work alongside those who not long before had been our enemies. They became my friends and I saw them as my equals.

I still had itchy feet and wanted to continue my career abroad. I even considered a teaching career within the education department of one of the armed services. As it worked out, I headed back to the UK to teach in a girls' boarding school—Christ's Hospital. My exploration of the world was put on hold, though with a possible option to take off again, under the umbrella of the Air Ministry, to teach in the international school for the children of NATO personnel, which had its headquarters at that time in Fontainebleau near Paris.

Epilogue

When I left the UK to live in Germany, I had what I then considered to be a strong and meaningful faith with a close personal relationship with God. It was my intention that once I had begun to settle down, I would seek out a German church with the opportunity to get to know some of the congregation. I hoped too that it might have a dual purpose in helping my spoken German, which had remained stagnant since my school days. I soon located a suitable church close to the school, but sadly I didn't feel particularly at home there. I enjoyed the singing but my limited knowledge of the language was a distinct barrier and I began to feel a bit of a loner within the congregation. After a few weeks I decided to give up. I turned my attention to the school to see what it offered in the area of worship and Christian fellowship.

Padre Tewkesbury was our school chaplain and he would normally take the Sunday morning services in the school chapel. The robed choir looked impressive as they proudly led the procession up the aisle. The service itself was Matins taken from the Book of Common Prayer. It reminded me of our Anglican college chapel service in Cheltenham, which I attended for Holy Communion on Sunday mornings. I valued these liturgical services.

Sadly, I no longer had the opportunity to teach the religious education which I enjoyed and for which I had been trained, as this subject was in the hands of the Padre.

I appreciated the company of my colleagues, although I missed the Christian fellowship I enjoyed back at home. However, I was set on making the most of all that the school was able to offer me, including that of making new friends.

It is true that I had previously lived quite a sheltered life. Now I was working and socialising with those who had wider experiences of life and its pleasures. I was (and still am) a person with a need to feel at home and accepted, feeling most comfortable with just one or two people who are like-minded.

Ideally, I needed a soulmate on my wavelength, an empathetic listener with whom I could share life, including my faith, with ease. Looking back now to those early days at King Alfred School, I ask myself why I didn't go to our chaplain, but I was hindered by my reserved and shy nature. I would have discussed with him the question of the 'legalism' to which I had been introduced soon after my conversion to Christianity.

Legalism hadn't been an issue at college. If we had a spiritual concern, there was always another at hand with whom we could toss it around using the truths of the Bible's teaching as our foundation. Now in a different environment in Germany, worldly, seemingly innocent pleasures emerged. Devoid of any meaningful Christian fellowship, and being young in the faith, my trust in God and my love of him began to lose its joy and sparkle. With the benefit of hindsight, I realise that my faith may not have been sufficiently deep-rooted and was being tested over that period when I was experiencing so many mind-blowing cultural changes in my relatively young life whilst living in Occupied Germany. Could my Christian faith then perhaps be compared to a garden needing gentle tending and serious watering in order for it to thrive and grow? I know there was much that I gained and valued emotionally and mentally, but sadly I didn't grow spiritually. So often at any stage in a Christian's life we need a gentle reminder that Christian maturity can be characterised by the nine-fold fruit of the Spirit which Paul identifies in his letter to the Galatians:

Love, joy, peace, forbearance, kindness,
goodness, faithfulness, gentleness, self-control.
Against such things there is no law. (Galatians 5 v 22, 23)

The entrance to King Alfred School was manned 24/7

Quarter deck where a flag was raised and lowered
on a daily basis every morning and evening

Quarter deck with its bell rung signalling
the end of each lesson

Plaque to commemorate the planting of
the Sevenoaks oak tree

Formal planting of the oak tree in 1998

End of term 'Auf Wiedersehn' as pupils depart
on the school train to take them to their homes scattered
across the British zone of Occupied Germany

Awaiting the arrival of the school train

CHAPTER 7

Christ's Hospital, 1957–1958

I thrive on privilege and the unusual! This was something I experienced both in Germany and then at Christ's Hospital. It was a well-renowned public boarding school dating back to the sixteenth century, to which I was appointed to the teaching staff in 1957. At that time, Christ's Hospital was located in Hertford, and for girls only. Formerly it had been co-educational but, in 1902, the boys had moved to a grand new building in Horsham, Sussex where it is today. The Hertford site was closed in 1985, the girls transferred to Horsham, and once again it became a co-educational school. Today it has 900 pupils aged between 11 and 18, with an equal number of boys and girls. It is one of the oldest schools in the country and heavily endowed, offering first-class education to orphans or the fatherless, giving the pupils the stability needed for everyday life and on into adulthood, with opportunities to reach their full potential. Whilst I was at the school a very high percentage gained places at university, mostly to Oxford. I loved teaching there and valued the opportunity of being a part of such a unique school where I could play my part in the youngsters' development.

I have just found on the top of my bookcase a hardback book of the history of Christ's Hospital. Nostalgically for me, on the inside front cover, and in my father's own distinctive writing, is his signature 'BJ Saunders' followed by the date of 1953. This was four years before I joined the staff of the school. He was a great hoarder of books so he may already have had it on his bookshelf and given it to me when I was appointed to the school, or maybe I had acquired it in the interim period leading up to his death in 1975. The book has a wealth of information about the school, together with quotes from well-known former students such as Samuel Taylor Coleridge.

When I arrived in 1957 the school had only had three headmistresses since the boys moved to Horsham in 1902—the year of Queen Victoria's jubilee. The third of these was Miss West, my headmistress, who was appointed in 1942 and served until 1972—30 years of service!

I loved its historical foundation, how it came into being and all those involved. The school was first opened in 1552 to 380 pupils drawn from the poor of London. King Edward VI played a leading role in its founding when, responding to an 'impassioned' sermon by Nicholas Ridley, Bishop of London, he felt the call to focus on the needs of London's underprivileged children. With the help of the Lord Mayor of London at the time, an old building vacated by Grey Friars in Newgate was bought, into which pupils of all ages were admitted. It not only provided learning for the fatherless, but also met the urgent need for clothing, food and lodging. During the Middle Ages, hospitals served different functions. Medieval hospitals were not just hospitals in their own right but had alms houses for the poor and hostels for pilgrims. Christ's Hospital embraced all. The care they provided helped to prepare each resident for their future careers. Although it was initially for boys only, just 11 years later, in 1563, its doors were opened to girls as well. At that time a third of all pupils were girls. Shortly before the King's death in 1553, the school received a royal charter signed by the King himself.

Tragedy came when 37 children lost their lives in the Plague of London of 1665. (Comparison can be made with the tragic loss of young lives in WW2 and in the recent Covid pandemic.) A year later, in 1666, the Grey Friars building situated near St Paul's Cathedral was severely damaged in the Great Fire of London and was no longer habitable. Arrangements were made for these young people to be billeted in nearby Hertfordshire. Their forced move from London reminds me of the compulsory evacuations of so many children from London in 1940 when East London suffered devastating bombing and loss of life in the Blitz.

A large, self-contained building was found on the outskirts of Hertford and became the new residence of Christ's Hospital, where it was owned and run as a co-educational boarding school for the next 300 years.

The ethos of the school remains today. It is still run on the lines that no child is excluded in situations when the parents or guardians have insufficient funds to pay the fees, with the balance found from other resources.

Bluecoat School, as it has been called for its distinctive dress, is full of traditions, one of which I do remember clearly. An important day in the school calendar is St Matthew's Day (21 September) marking the day on which, from at least 1557, the names of the governors of the Royal Hospitals of St Bartholomew's, Christ's, Bridewell, Bethlem and St Thomas's were given to the Lord Mayor for ceremonial approval. To this day, pupils from Christ's Hospital School maintain a long-established tradition by processing from the Church of St Sepulchre Newgate Street through the City of London to the Guildhall, where they partake of luncheon with the Lord Mayor of London. The school choir, band and senior pupils traditionally travel to London on a date close to 21 September for a service in a City of London church, on which occasion they receive a largesse (gift) from the Lord Mayor. Christ's Hospital has always maintained a close relationship with both royalty and the City of London.

During my time in the school seven of us were accommodated in a house owned by the school, conveniently located a few steps across the road from the school complex. My memory here is a bit hazy, but I think we were responsible for our own breakfast, with lunch prepared and provided for us in the house. For dinner we joined the rest of the staff in the dining hall in the main school.

At Christ's Hospital, with fewer responsibilities or duties outside the classroom, I had time to myself and was able to lead a more independent life than in Germany.

I was delighted to make friends with a dear person of strong character and Christian faith. Although we had different backgrounds and experiences of life, we related well and enjoyed each other's company. We were able to visit local places of interest together, and on 'high days and holidays' I would drop her off at the door of her home near Wembley before driving on to my parents in Kent. Our friendship made such a valuable contribution to this particular period in my life. She accepted my thirst for adventure and the unusual but it was almost beyond her comprehension.

I was appointed to teach general subjects to the 10–14-year-olds: English language and literature, maths, geography and religious education. The girls were so eager to learn, and I found the work satisfying and fulfilling. I was delighted to play my small part in preparing them for university and their future lives.

Following tradition, the school was divided into wards (not houses) with its own ward mistress whose sole responsibility was to care for all the children's needs outside the classroom, including meals. Enforced letter writing took place in the wards on Sunday afternoons, when it was required that they each write to their parents or guardians, handing these over to the ward mistress for posting. One of our few duties as teachers was to accompany compulsory crocodile walks around the town. I would turn a blind eye to those in the crocodile who, in their desire for privacy, chose to post letters surreptitiously as we passed the distinctive red-letter boxes!

There were other negatives and rules with which I and others didn't agree, such as the fact that the girls had virtually no contact with boys. The one exception was a formal dinner held at the end of each term to which boys from a neighbouring school were invited.

Why did I leave unexpectedly after just a year? Basically, I put this down to the fact that the school had been under the same headship for close on 20 years and the traditions and rules were outdated.

At the end of each term, in a designated room, reports were written and left there for the next person. This, I accepted and understood. By tradition reports were written in ink in a beautiful leather-bound book with the grade for each subject needing to be written in different coloured inks according to the effort made. I had no option but to follow the rules.

However, my downfall came at the end of my second term! Mother would say that, unlike Mary, I wasn't the most careful of beings as I was always keen to move on and do the next thing. I think my error was in not using the correct colour of ink. Although I tried my best to erase it, the error was clearly very noticeable and I knew it would be unacceptable! It was an error on my part which I obviously accepted. However, I was angry with both the protocol of the system and with myself for making the error. Near perfection was expected of us and I had failed.

What to do? I felt like a naughty schoolgirl! It was 9 o'clock at night. Undeterred, I wrote a brief note to the headmistress handing in my notice, not giving the reason, and put it through her personal letter box at her residence. I remember all that so clearly.

I had originally planned to stay at Christ's Hospital for a couple of years. However, I knew that if there were to be a vacancy at the International School in Fontainebleau in September, that might now be worth considering.

Epilogue

When I arrived at Christ's Hospital, I had a longing to embrace a meaningful faith again and for God's hand to be there for me along my spiritual journey, giving me the nourishment needed to grow spiritually as a Christian.

The time was ripe to adjust to life in an environment with its Christian foundation and draw God back into my life. This Christian tradition at the school was of a more orthodox nature than I would have liked but not without its spiritual dimension. There was a daily chapel service at the start of the day which I normally attended. As the scriptures were read and the Lord's Prayer said, I had an opportunity to draw closer to God and reflect on where I was in my relationship with him. I was beginning to see that life without him was one without purpose and hope. I needed God's guiding hand and for him to become 'Lord' of my life.

My regular visits to my parents for weekends and holidays began to mean a lot to me. They were then living in the beautiful Kent countryside in the village of Shoreham. I would attend the morning Sunday service with my father either at the village church or the parish church in nearby Sevenoaks, which later in my life became my 'home' church. This might be followed by a drink at a village pub before returning to their cottage to enjoy a meal faithfully and well-prepared by my mother. Although rarely speaking about his personal faith, my father didn't treat Christianity lightly, having great respect for those of faith and the genuineness of mine; deep down his own meant a lot to him and was much a part of who he was. He was unaware at the time that he too played a role in my journey of faith and was there for me a few years later following the tragic loss of a loved one—the love of my life.

Two of the clauses in the Christ's Hospital Mission statement read:

'To present to its pupils the Christian faith in all its mystery and splendour', and this was truly evident in the overall Christian ethos of the school.

'To have regard especially to children of families in social, financial or other need, in the choice of pupils, that choice to remain the prerogative of the Foundation'. I was conscious that the school adhered to this closely, with everyone treated equally irrespective of background.

The school's definitive Christian foundation was such that most traditional events in the life of the school opened with prayer.

I am grateful for all I learned through my experiences during that year at Christ's Hospital, which has played its part in shaping my future. My love for God had deepened and despite my failings I had a clearer understanding of his unfailing love for me. I was in a better place on my spiritual journey and ready to move on to new pastures.

CHAPTER 8

A Taste of France, 1958–1963

It was late August 1958, at the time when Charles de Gaulle was president of France, that I drew up in my Morris Minor outside 30 Rue Royale with some trepidation. The street was so named as, in the distant past, royalty would have driven along it to reach the famous Chateau of Fontainebleau. With relief that my journey was over, I parked my car on the road outside and approached the house only to be confronted with massive iron gates, which were locked. My only option was to ring the bell to gain entry. The owner of the house soon appeared, taking me along the long path to the main door and up the stairs to my garret apartment on the third floor. This area was to be shared with a gentleman from Tunisia who had arrived a few months earlier to escape the bombing of his homeland by the French. I was not too happy with the prospect of sharing the facilities with him but as I had no option, I just accepted it.

At that time personnel from Canada, USA, Belgium, the Netherlands, and the UK served at the Supreme HQ of the Allied Powers Europe (SHAPE), which had its NATO HQ in

Fontainebleau. I and my British colleagues were employed by the Air Ministry. Here I was yet again signing the Official Secrets Act.

My life in Fontainebleau was 'chalk and cheese' compared with King Alfred School in Germany, but I valued the contrast that each was able to offer. Instead of teaching secondary aged pupils in a boarding school, I would be teaching in the primary department of an all-age day school. The British pupils and staff were accommodated in prefabricated classrooms erected in the grounds of the International Lycée, overseen by the Directeur, Monsieur du Pré. Like it or not, he was the boss of us all and we were required to attend the Lycée staff meetings. Since these were in French, and I invariably had difficulty understanding what was being said, I would switch off! Most of our meetings were to do with the *French* pupils' behaviour.

The pressure of work was much less intense than at the school in Germany. For instance, there were no lessons at weekends! I welcomed the opportunity to have more of a social life. Having taught in two boarding schools over the previous four years it was somewhat of a relief to be in a day school, giving me greater freedom to live my life 'my way'.

We were required to supervise our own classes during morning breaks and to accompany those who weren't going home that day for lunch on the coach to NATO HQ a couple of miles away where they would have their midday meal. My timetable was such that, on two afternoons a week,

I was released from my own class to teach English to French senior aged pupils in the main building. Discipline at the senior school was exercised by 'surveillants', which in practice meant that when children misbehaved, they were told by their teacher to go into the corridor and await the approach and subsequent punishment from a 'surveillant', whose duty was to parade all the time up and down the corridors of the school. The punishment was often a physical one. I didn't want any child to suffer this indignity, so I preferred to exercise my own judgement and punishment within the classroom.

I loved the teaching and valued no longer being bound too much to the curricula. Our British headmaster was quite laid back and trusted us as experienced teachers to follow our instincts that were in the best interests of the pupils.

I related well to our junior department staff; we had four classes—one for each year group—normally with between 30 and 40 pupils in each. Those who taught the secondary age group were mostly highly specialised teachers and able to offer a range of subjects in which they were well qualified and experienced, including Greek and Latin. Here the teaching groups were small, as at that stage in their education a number of pupils would move on, sometimes to boarding schools back in the UK. Contracts for NATO personnel tended to be longer than those of service personnel in Occupied Germany, which meant those who continued at the school for longer had every chance of reaching their own potential.

Now back to my life away from the school. I certainly wasn't happy with my shared garret accommodation: poor cooking facilities, a shared bathroom, countless stairs and, with a long front drive to the iron entrance gate. No-one could pop in to visit me without needing to ring the bell at these formidable gates, often a deterrent for the visitor to come at all. I seemed cut off from the outside world.

That autumn to my dismay countless mosquitoes appeared, taking great delight in their constant attack on my poor body. I would be covered with bites and frequently kept awake at night; my walls were marked with blood stains of those that I had managed to annihilate! Not a pleasant memory!

On the positive side, the house was located on Rue Royale, the most prestigious street in Fontainebleau, and within walking distance of the town, the forest, and the chateau. Opposite the house was the British officers' mess, which we were at liberty to use, so I would enjoy the occasional meal there and join others for Scottish dancing on Tuesday evenings.

In less than a year I was delighted to make a move into a first-floor self-contained apartment in a typical stone-built, three-storey, semi-detached house just a few metres from the centre of the town. It was convenient for shops and the twice weekly market as well as the many street terrace cafes, bars and small restaurants located in the town's main street, Rue Grande, for a coffee or a tempting prix fixe meal and taste of local French wine. A few years ago, I returned with friends to visit my old haunts; very little seemed to have changed. My favourite cafe was still there and as popular as ever; I was thankful to discover the loos had been upgraded!

From my new apartment the main entrance to the chateau was only a couple of hundred metres away. As staff working for NATO, we had the privilege of attending cocktail parties and special events in the chateau's beautifully appointed and renowned ballroom. These occasions I would normally attend but I am never at my ease and comfortable standing around, sipping cocktails and trying to socialise with folk I don't know. My preference would be to sit unnoticed just as an onlooker!

The street where I lived was narrow; one could almost shake hands with those who lived opposite! On hot summer Sundays we would open our street windows and the strains of popular songs of the time such as 'Never on Sunday!' would be heard; it created a distinctive and for me such an enjoyable ambience, typifying the French way of life. What an uproar there would be amongst my neighbours in my small conclave of houses and cottages in Sevenoaks if I dared to do so now!

An original painting of Moret-sur-Loing hangs with pride of place in my sitting room. The picture depicts the bridge across the River Loing, a tributary of the Seine with the medieval Église de la Nativité in the background, said to be France's smallest cathedral. As I glance across at the painting, it brings back memories of a number of unforgettable evenings spent with friends at a Michelin recommended restaurant overlooking the river. On my first occasion there were just two of us. The wine, a Chateau Neuf du Pape, soon became my favourite. But what I recall so clearly was the special ambience that was created for us . We were on the same wavelength such that a deep and meaningful conversation flowed—something I valued so much but rarely experienced, and one that I long for even now. I subsequently spent many happy evenings in that restaurant with other friends; conversations would flow, but none quite equalled that first one!

I loved the prospect of going out in the evening for a meal with a friend to enjoy the atmosphere of a typical small French restaurant. In Fontainebleau there was a plethora of restaurants scattered around the narrow streets and alleys and with so much choice that we would spend time comparing the prix fixe menus displayed outside before making our decision. Depending on how we were feeling on the day, we might select a restaurant with an intimate and quiet atmosphere or alternatively one with a lot of buzz. Choosing was an excitement in itself. If in the right mood and I couldn't find another person to accompany me, undeterred I would head off even on my own, and enjoy the experience!

Possessing a car was a 'must'! One weekend, as I was driving around the countryside, I came across a small private airfield which both intrigued me and, with my adventurous spirit, tickled my fancy. It displayed a large 'défense d'entrée notice; I was intrigued so I later consulted my NATO colleagues to enquire about it. To my delight, I discovered it offered both gliding and flying lessons. I was all for it! First, there was a rigorous medical health examination, before which I wisely refused an after-dinner cognac and then, with my provisional flying licence in hand, I was up in the air for my first lesson – a truly exhilarating experience!

I soon became aware that members of the club were mostly male and had a wartime background in the RAF. Knowing that these pilots had actually flown Spitfires meant I was in awe of them. I used to hang around the hangars like a child observing these experienced pilots, as they manually pushed the planes preparing them for flight. In no uncertain terms, they soon told me that I must play my part and so I did! I would watch these former wartime pilots in a side-by-side two-seater Piper plane, performing aerobatics, treating it as if it were a Spitfire. Memories and visions of the courage of such pilots in the Battle of Britain came flooding back to me.

It was a fantastic experience to be flying over the vast Forêt de Fontainebleau, identifying the villages along the river Seine banks. At one moment I was taxi-ing around that small airport from the runway towards the hangar, and then within a few minutes I needed to adapt from flying a plane to driving my car. I would find myself intuitively assuming the gear lever was the joystick and treating it as such and wondering why there was no lift-off! A strange phenomenon!

Flying lessons were in French, which I found was a bit of a hindrance as my knowledge of the language was somewhat limited. After 50 hours of flying time, I was considered ready to fly solo. I walked across the runway with my instructor for the plane's final preparations for take-off, my head buzzing with numerous 'ifs' running around my brain. Was I actually ready to do this, bearing in mind that my lessons had been in French? What would happen if something went wrong with the plane and in my fear, I forgot what I was supposed to do? What would happen if I had difficulty in landing and needed to try, try, try again?

As I was about to climb into the cockpit, I chickened out. I knew I would feel and be seen as a fool. I didn't want that. I made the excuse even to myself that flying was too expensive a hobby for me to keep up, which was true. However, it was my fear and lack of confidence that was nearer the truth. I do have a few regrets at my decision, and of not being equal to the challenge.

My adventurous spirit would very occasionally rear its head after school on a Friday at the start of the weekend, when, with no immediate plans, I would quickly pack a small travel bag, climb into my car, and make my way to regions not so far away such as the Loire Valley. Towards nightfall I would look for a quiet and quaint auberge and there I would enjoy a simple meal of whatever was on offer with a glass or two of red wine, and then spend the night in a not-so comfortable bed.

These auberges seemed to exude that same unique French ambience which I relished in more ways than one! Whether I genuinely enjoyed these jaunts on my own I will never really know. What I do know was that I didn't want to become a 'stick in the mud'. France was on my doorstep and I wanted to make the most of my opportunities and explore other parts of the country, even if this meant doing it on my own.

In my eyes, Paris is almost equal to London. Each has so much to offer. Unlike bomb damaged London, Paris had remained virtually unscathed due to its capitulation to the Germans in 1940.

Paris became my regular haunt on Sundays. Nostalgia sets in as I give glimpses of how I spent those Sundays in the city, one that had so much to offer with choices to be made as to how to spend them.

The first choice was whether to travel by car or by train. The train to the Gare de Lyon took less than an hour; the downside was that Fontainebleau Station was two miles away with limited parking facilities. By road the journey would be just over an hour (traffic permitting). Although there were occasions when I would go on my own, I normally went with a colleague I knew well, going in his car. Starting on the Route N7 (the main road by-passing Fontainebleau), our route would take us alongside the forest, past Barbizon, the artists' paradise, and passing Orly airport to the right into the suburbs of Paris and into the heart of the city.

The next choice was how we would spend the day. Sometimes, if we had made an early start, we would seek out a church and attend the morning service; since my colleague spoke Russian and was familiar with church orthodoxy, our choice whittled down to the Russian Orthodox church or St Michael's Church, an English-speaking Anglican church in the diocese of Europe. Both were on the Right Bank of the River Seine. I remember that there were no seats in the Russian church so we had to stand; the service was led by a priest who stood in the front of the Holy of Holies but I didn't warm to his monotonal voice in a language I didn't understand. St Michael's Church offered us boxed pews with hard wooden seats, but it was a service that I understood and enjoyed.

Sometimes we would start our time in Paris at a cafe in the area of Les Halles, renowned for its food market which over many years had met the needs of the poor. After a quick look and shop around the market we might set off for Montmartre, which occupied a position high above the city with astonishing, extensive views over the capital. We parked the car in one of the narrow streets close to the funicular railway, which we took to the top. The highest point of Montmartre is the nineteenth century Basilica of the Sacre Coeur, which we might pop into before making our way to the very heart of Montmartre to the Place du Tertre, an artist's paradise, where we would wander around, watching the painters at work. In the centre of the square, waiters from restaurants around the square's periphery were always busy serving meals at the tables there, meeting the culinary needs of visitors like us. Although not an historical area of Paris I still have happy memories of Montmartre with all it offered, and no doubt still does!

A visit to a museum or art gallery proved to be a 'must'. The pact I made was that these visits were to be little and often. In other words, to spend just a short time savouring a particular treasure, such as the 'Mona Lisa' in the Louvre or Rodin's famous sculpture of 'The Thinker' in the Gardens of Rodin, returning for more another day.

My own favourite was heading to the Musée de l'Orangerie at the Tuileries Gardens near the Concorde, to see Monet's famous water lilies, with its impressive length of 100 metres and beautifully displayed in two elliptical rooms. Such a feeling of peace and tranquillity came over me as I viewed and studied the painting. I subsequently had a similar experience when visiting Monet's gardens near Giverny, which became a regular haunt of mine such that in later years when in the travel business, I found myself organising and escorting groups there.

Sometimes we would choose to go directly to the Left Bank, have coffee in the area of St-Germain-des-Prés and then settle down for a leisurely lunch in a quiet back street, ending the afternoon at the cinema to see a carefully chosen recent film. In the late fifties and early sixties there was an amazing choice of new and popular films shown at the plethora of cinemas found along the streets of St-Germain-des-Prés. Paris is a wonderful city and is still dear to my heart.

Towards the end of my second year in France, I bought a touring caravan which I towed from the Channel port to Fontainebleau, and to a camping site in the forest. My objective was to take it down to a site located near the sea, above Antibes and not far from St Paul de Vence. Mother kindly came over to join me on that first drive south. She didn't drive so it was all up to me. As she watched me hoist the small, seemingly heavy towbar of the touring caravan onto the car, she remarked, 'Wend, you will suffer for this one day!'

On that first occasion I gingerly drove very slowly, hesitating to overtake another vehicle, quietly cheering the first time when we did. I loved it when friends from the UK joined me for these holidays in the south. Zoe, a friend who enjoyed the comforts of her flat in Kensington, on a couple of occasions, travelled down first-class by train to Nice, where I met her and settled her into a hotel in St Paul de Vence. She thoroughly enjoyed these holidays. Other friends joined us and camped close by. We were aware when she joined us for meals on a camp site that these were not quite her kettle of fish!

By French law, I was not permitted to rent the caravan out for financial gain. As I did not want it to remain empty during term time, I offered it to friends who would just pay me for their expenses. Towards the end of my five years living in France, I towed it back, first to the same site in the forest of Fontainebleau, and then to a four-star site high up on the cliffs overlooking the English Channel just east of St Malo. Here, when all was quiet and we had settled down for the night the gentle sounds of the waves across the shore beneath could be heard. I loved this location for the caravan and from time to time would drive up to spend a weekend there with friends and on one occasion with my mother. It was then towards the end of my time in France that I hoisted the towbar onto the caravan, crossed the Channel to Dover and left it on a site on the cliffs overlooking the port. Eventually I plucked up courage and towed it to Scotland, where it finished its days in Aviemore—sadly abandoned on a campsite! It was all well worthwhile, for I know the ways in which the caravan had given so much pleasure to me and so many others over the years!

For the last couple of years during my time in Fontainebleau I lived in a bungalow built in the grounds of a large house on the edge of the forest. It was a wise and practical move, and an improvement on the town apartment, apart from it being a ten-minute walk to the shops. It was detached with two bedrooms, a large living room, spacious kitchen, bathroom and even an attached garage. Just across the road 100 metres away in one direction was the edge of the forest. Just opposite the bungalow there was Fontainebleau's minor injuries hospital, giving that feeling of reassurance if I were to have an emergency. I recall using its services once when I carelessly scalded myself.

I enjoyed the space and peace the bungalow offered, which enabled me to do more entertaining, which I much enjoyed. I was able to create a play-reading group and we would regularly meet every couple of weeks. It was no longer a problem to accommodate visitors from the UK.

After my extended five-year contract with the Air Ministry ended, I returned in 1963 to live for the first time in London. That five-year period in France was truly memorable for me. I know I had been enriched intellectually, mentally, emotionally, and spiritually too mainly through the special and supportive friendships I made. I had experienced a varied and action-packed life in a country that I had grown to love. I know I matured as an individual during those five years there and learned to live a deeper and more fulfilled life. Looking back now it was a time that played a strategic role in shaping my future. Did I learn to live life more 'abundantly'? My reflections in the epilogues will answer that question.

Epilogue

Paul writes in the book of Philippians: 'one thing I do know: forgetting what lies behind and straining forward to what lies ahead, I press on toward the goal for the prize of the upward call of God in Christ Jesus.'

'Pressing on' is so much part of Paul's teaching in the New Testament. Throughout those five years in France, I pressed on in a worldly sense, enjoying the normal pleasures of life, but the goal was absent and my spiritual life was still not deep-rooted. I may have attended church services held regularly on the NATO complex, Paris and elsewhere, but sadly, in those early days I made little progress in my spiritual journey whilst attending them.

However, I know that God hadn't abandoned me, and I was given glimmers of hope that meant so much to me in my last year. Through our regular play- reading evenings held in my bungalow, I became friendly with a delightful couple,

Martyn Allies, our education officer and his wife, Lily. Since they played a significant role at different stages in my life, it is appropriate that I write a few words about them and their background.

Martyn had served as a fighter pilot for the RAF during the war, winning a number of awards and medals. In 1941, whilst on the shortest of his leaves, he and Lily were married—a quiet occasion with little time for any pomp or ceremony!

The Box of Beautiful Letters is a book written by his daughter, Cheryl, published only a short while ago. It is a wartime love story between Lily Smith and RAF pilot Martyn Allies, a story written between the two of them between 1939 and 1941 – and found within love letters she unearthed in their house and had kept for many years, hesitant about even reading them let alone for them to be published. After much heart searching, she decided that there was little to be lost in doing so and much to be gained.

Martyn, as our appointed education officer in Fontainebleau, was very conscientious, frequently going far beyond the call of duty, offering a variety of initiatives to all of us in the field of education, which were much valued and practised. Their youngest child, Bob, was in my class at the school at the time. He was a lovely, lively lad so eager to learn and a joy to teach. He became a well-known and respected architect in London and we are still in touch, exchanging cards at Christmas.

Martyn and Lily each had a quiet and genuine Christian faith, which they put into action in their everyday lives.

They did this with an attitude of humility that was evident in the way they treated everyone with respect and equality. During my last few months teaching in France, they had moved from a delightful home in an outlying village into an apartment within the town of Fontainebleau. At their invitation I began to spend more time in their company enabling me to witness their faith in action in a very real way: they unwittingly scattered seeds for me along my own journey of faith, which bore their fruit in later years. It was a privilege and delight to know them. Over the decades I spent many happy times in their company until Martyn died aged 89 in 2010, and a few years later Lily joined him. In his later years and now myself following suit, I recall so clearly Martyn saying that he didn't recommend old age!

Since my early years I knew that God had given me life to be enjoyed, but I only gradually began to fully comprehend that this 'joie de vivre' needs to be rooted within one's relationship with God and stems from him. We read in John's gospel some beautiful words, which I was yet fully to grasp and own:

I came that they may have life
And that they may have it more abundantly.
(John 10 v 10)

Wendy stands close to the entrance of the L' Ecole
Internationale where for five years she taught the children
of NATO personnel stationed in Fontainebleau

The Allies' family (Martyn and Lily with Cheryl and Bob) outside
their house in Marlotte not far from Fontainebleau. Wendy
remained close friends with the family over many decades

A Latin class in the Lycee

Front of the Lycee

Back of Lycee

Moret-sur-Loing with me. This delightful dreamy
medieval village lies on the edge of the Foret de Fontainebleau.
Wendy has many a happy memory of romantic meals
taken alongside waterfront restaurants.

Wendy's father aged 81 enjoying the delights of
Moret-sur Loing during his week's holiday

Our larders were stocked from this popular market
in the centre of Fontainebleau

CHAPTER 9

London in the Sixties, 1963–1968

The decade of the sixties was dominated politically by the Vietnam War and the Cuban Missile Crisis. It saw the assassinations of two notable Americans—US President John F Kennedy in 1963 and Martin Luther King, the Baptist minister, spokesperson, and leader of the Civil Rights Movement. Another landmark event was England's victory over Germany in 1966 in the World Cup. The decade ended on another good note when the first man landed on the moon. All this I recall as if it were yesterday; I would follow the news on the radio, in the newspapers and also on my very first television screen.

The Swinging Sixties was a youth-driven, cultural revolution that had at its core modernity and fun. It saw a flourishing in art, music and fashion, and was symbolised by the iconic pop and fashion exports. At the age of just 32, I moved straight from France into that contrasting culture and was somewhat mesmerised by it.

Shortly before I left France and with little optimism, I applied for a post at Coborn Grammar School for Girls in

Bow in the east end of London. I assumed I would need to return to the UK if I were called for interview, but to my surprise the interview was conducted by phone, but at our local bureau de poste. In those days most people had no personal landline telephone let alone a mobile. A letter soon followed offering me the post. I would be teaching mainly maths up to O-level and also have special responsibility to manage and oversee the school stationery! I jumped at this job. So that is where I taught and lived for the next five years. Looking back, I now see that it was the right school for me at the time. I loved the teaching, got on well with the other staff and made some long-lasting friendships.

I lived for a couple of years in a more than acceptable, modern, well-located, rented apartment in Chalk Farm, close to both Hampstead and Regent's Park. Popping casually into a pub for a drink and a snack in Hampstead on a Saturday morning on my own didn't daunt me; it was, in fact, a pleasant distraction from everyday life. Likewise, I loved the peace and beauty of a Sunday morning stroll in nearby Regent's Park. On occasions I would enjoy attending an evening performance of a Shakespeare play in its open-air theatre.

Coborn and Coopers were state schools affiliated to a Coopers livery company. Prisca Coborn, or 'Cobourne' (1622–1701), was the widow of a Bow brewer, who left property at Bow, Stratford and Bocking, Essex. She opened a school for a maximum of 50 poor children in premises there. The boys were to learn reading, writing and accounts, and the girls reading, writing and needlework. Two centuries later at the end of the nineteenth century, Coopers, the boys' school, moved to other premises close by and the two schools remained separate until just three years after I left. Then both schools moved to Upminster in Essex, merging into a co-ed comprehensive secondary school, still a popular and thriving school today. Like Christ's Hospital, Coborn thus had an historical start to its life.

In my first year there, in addition to my maths teaching, I was asked to teach French to first-year pupils. This was a role I didn't relish as my French wasn't up to it! Individual speech therapy lessons, which I took at lunch times, were more my cup of tea.

A number of Jewish families had settled in Bow as a result of the war. Once in school there seemed little divide between those who were Jewish and those who were likely to have lived all their lives in the local area. I was bemused by the way the Jewish pupils had two ways to speak: 'lazy' English at home and 'proper' Queen's English at school!

I found the pupils as eager to learn as I was to teach. I was as anxious as they were each year as we awaited the O-level results. These proved to be beyond my personal expectations. I am not a mathematician nor an academic but the gift that God has given me is the ability to be on a youngster's wavelength, able to iron out with them aspects of the subject where they lacked understanding, often in the area of algebra. From time to time in later years, I have offered tuition in my own home to those struggling at school; more often than not they needed to build up their confidence.

At Coborn I related well with the headmistress, Miss Legerton, although I hadn't quite shaken off my shyness with those in authority. She was an excellent head, much respected and liked by staff and pupils alike, having the relevant gifts that were needed to run the school in an effective way. There were sadly two or three somewhat crusty and crotchety individuals on the teaching staff, who seemed to be constantly grumbling and criticising, which went against the grain for most of us.

Miss Legerton was especially kind and understanding to me when, towards the end of my first year, I suffered the loss of a former colleague and true soulmate. He had been ill with a blood condition for several months and now I had to understand and absorb the fact that our life together was not to be. Bereaved himself as a young child, his education had been in a seminary. When the war came he felt called to play his part and to serve his country, so his calling to the priesthood was thwarted. I was encouraged to take a break from school, which initially I was reluctant to do; I wanted to be stoic but that wasn't to be.

Endeavouring in that first year at Coborn to sweep my bereavement under the carpet, and not having lived in London previously, I wanted to explore what this capital city in the sixties had to offer.

Maybe I wasn't quite into the 'Swing' of the sixties but I loved taking the underground into its centre or from time to time driving around it in my Wolseley 1500. I started to make friends who had common interests with me and would regularly go with one or two of them to concerts at the Royal Festival Hall or to the theatre. Restaurants in London at that time were in no way equal to those I had experienced in France, but to join with others for meals at weekends was still part of my weekly agenda and much enjoyed.

I had to accept the fact that there was an enormous gap in my life following my bereavement. Could this in time be filled through an acquaintance I made with a delightful neighbour. We related well together and conversations developed on to that deep level and helped to fill that needy gap in me. We would discuss at length my own Christian faith and what it meant to me as well as Christianity as a whole, which was absent in his own life.

Unexpectedly one evening he told me he had just been selected and offered a new opportunity of a job in Libya that had great prospects of enhancing his career. He suggested I went with him in order to give us more time to get to know one another better and not to be hasty in any decision we might make. I was tempted but it was a radical decision for me to make and I knew its timing wasn't ripe for me to make. I reluctantly declined. Hesitating himself but realising that at the age of 30 his career needed to come first, he accepted the post. It was with deep disappointment, on both sides, that we parted saying at the same time that it would be for the best if we made no further contact with each other.

Teaching proved to be a diversion and in school I was able to function relatively well. However, my mental condition began to deteriorate and in the last year at Coborn I was diagnosed with clinical depression. Still in my mid-thirties, I was ill-prepared. I suffered an indescribable aloneness and lost purpose in life. The main symptom was one of uncontrollable crying. Margaret, a colleague who became a special and close friend, was my mainstay even though she was not without her own problems. It was Margaret who suggested I seek professional help.

It is appropriate now to say that my special friendship with Margaret left a positive legacy in my own life lasting for many decades. She and her husband Jeremy eventually left London to run a country restaurant near Taunton. I would be their frequent visitor. One of my special birthdays was celebrated there, with friends from around the country staying in local bed and breakfasts. Then, when she was only in her sixties, Margaret suffered an embolism and died. After Margaret's death, I kept in contact with Jeremy, who sadly suffered clinical depression, never really getting over his loss.

Just as it did with Jeremy, my own bereavement and depression went hand in hand. Following Margaret's advice, I consulted my GP, who referred me to a psychologist, with whom I had several sessions. Understanding the seriousness of my condition, he gave me 'carte blanche' to phone him any time I felt I could no longer cope. This was my lifeline. Regrettably, the time came one Friday evening when I knew I needed help. I phoned him and within a short while on that same evening I was admitted to a psychiatric hospital. With the school granting me a month's absence on medical grounds, I spent the next five weeks at Halliwick.

Halliwick Hospital, built in the grounds of Friern Hospital, opened in 1958 as a neurosis unit with 145 beds, primarily for those with professional backgrounds. 'Certified' patients continued to be treated in Friern Hospital. The hospital to which I was admitted had a visionary approach unlike other mental hospitals of the day. As a child I remember such places were called 'loony bins'.

A variety of treatments were offered: one-to-one talking therapy as well as group therapy in which some seven or eight people would meet daily overseen by a member of the hospital staff. The therapy I most valued and enjoyed and was the most absorbing, was centred around the weekly production of a hospital newspaper. Here I played an active role, writing articles and helping in the editing.

A third, more radical treatment was electroconvulsive therapy (ECT), which was used as a 'quick fix improvement' therapy. It was suggested that ECT would be appropriate for me. By that time, I felt a bit of a fraud being in the hospital at all; I found it difficult to acknowledge and accept that I was mentally ill. I was eager to have a 'quick fix', but I had not fully explored the implications of ECT, about which there is ongoing controversy. The procedure involves a general anaesthetic during which an electric current is passed through the brain. Upon regaining consciousness a few minutes later, one is disorientated with short term memory loss. I had three or four of these procedures. It was not pleasant, and was disorientating to say the least, but I accepted the fact that it was worth it, as I soon felt infinitely better. I valued the support of a fellow patient there who proved to be empathetic and understanding. With the benefit of hindsight, I am aware that I should have questioned more the potential permanent effects of ECT on my brain. I will never know what it did in the long term since I have no idea what I would have been like without it!

Towards the end of January 1968, I was discharged and, feeling so much better, I was able to return to school. I have recently found a letter from Miss Legerton, the headmistress, written in her own handwriting on 9 January wishing me well. I realise now how much she and the other staff cared for my well-being, which meant a lot to me. I felt so guilty at letting down the students, especially those in the fourth and fifth years preparing for their O-levels.

Epilogue

No tears—just a numbness and an unimaginable aloneness when the love of my life passed away. Deep down I knew God was there for me, but I needed friends to turn to for understanding and hugs. I even have tears running down my cheeks now as I recall finding two places of refuge. The first was to my dear faithful friends, Martyn and Lily, known so well from our days in France. That same day, a Sunday, when my dear, dear friend died peacefully in hospital, I arrived on their doorstep in Caversham near Reading. The other was from an unexpected source: that of my dear,

dear Father. I visited my parents a few days later and as I climbed out of my car and into the back garden, about to pass in front of Father's den where he worked away at his writing, I stopped in front of his window, stunned to see several candles burning merrily away on the inside windowsill. This for him was the means by which he was able to show his understanding and his deep affection for me. This seemed to symbolise light in the darkness of death with life and hope assured for the future. He was of high Anglican tradition where in church candles were the norm, but what they then personally communicated to me overwhelmed me. No need for words. He loved me, longed to take my hand through this devastating time of loss. Looking back now I do see him as instrumental in slowly leading me a few steps further and deeper into a more secure and deeper relationship with God.

Life is full of bereavements, with each experience of grief being unique for the person concerned. Friends may long to help but sadly sometimes in their enthusiasm may even aggravate the situation. I was desperate for friends and so valued those who with a Christian faith would draw alongside me not necessarily with words, but personifying the love of Jesus in the way they cared and understood what I was going through.

A man's heart plans his way, but the
LORD directs his steps.
(Proverbs 16 v 9)

PART 2

Contents

Introduction

I have many regrets about a number of the decisions I made during my early adulthood years. Not all were negative; some gave much pleasure, allowing me a wealth of interesting experiences and the opportunity to meet a variety of interesting people. In those moments of regret, there is a modicum of consolation as I reflect on how God picked me up from those muddy waters, forgave and restored me, leading me into new pastures and releasing me to focus on the present—no longer dwelling on the 'ifs' of life. Past experiences were not wasted but used to shape my personal development and subsequent ministries. I was able to draw from a pot which I was subconsciously creating in those earlier years and use them for the benefit of others. I see 'loving my neighbour' in a new light, teaching me day by day to be less self-seeking and egocentric.

Bereavements, especially when sudden and traumatic, are never forgotten but need to be woven into our lives. As you will have already read, this is a lesson I learned in my early thirties when my soulmate and the love of my life passed away.

Following my loss, five years later a lovely kind and caring person younger than me crossed my path and within a few months of meeting we had tied the knot for life, as we then envisaged. It was an unusually quiet ceremony with only immediate family and two friends attending. Each of us in our individual way felt alone with a longing to love and be loved; fulfilment was truly evident in our newly found relationship. John having started his adult life reading politics, philosophy, and economics at Oxford, for a variety of reasons, not least his love of rowing (!) gave up his studies there after his first year, something I think he regretted in later life. Within a short while he had joined the retail travel business. He was keen to start his own business so within a few months of our marriage we moved from London to live in Hythe on the coast of Kent where we started our own small travel agency sharing premises at first with a village post office. I soon began teaching again—part-time in a local secondary school to help keep us afloat financially.

The second part of this book describes how I entered into a people-centred life, serving initially as a bereavement counsellor and a trustee of a local Christian counselling service, followed by pastoral ministry in my parish church. Some years later my career changed from teaching into that of managing a retail travel agency. Here I was able to merge my Christian ministry into travel and start to organise and lead travel groups abroad, something I continued to do until 2019, long after I had sold the business. A full life I have to admit, but one into which I know God had prepared and called me.

Unlike Part One, it is shorter, not written in any particular chronological order, and each chapter will cover these specific areas of the next fifty-year period of my life, and how I had been shaped by the experiences of earlier years to serve and work in the way I did.

CHAPTER 1

Personal Travelogue

Travel is in my blood. I did so much during my long school holidays whilst teaching in Germany and France; first in my Morris Minor and subsequently in my Wolseley 1500, visiting almost all western European countries. Some of these trips were with friends, but most were solo! I recall picking up young hitchhikers (mostly students) for company, when feeling a bit bored and on the last leg of my drive back to Fontainebleau. Suffice it to say, I only stopped for those who were waving the Union Jack, thus identifying themselves as British. I came to no harm but I realise now that it was a bit risky!

It was exciting to take off in my car on these jaunts but at times the unexpected happened. Let me recount two experiences. The first was when I was living near the Russian zone of northern Occupied Germany and longing to take opportunities to become acquainted with the country in which I was living. One of my trips took me to the eastern part of Western Occupied Germany. Having meandered through delightful and peaceful villages, I quite unexpectedly came face to face with the Hungarian border, confronted by a notice sprawled across the road with the words: *Es ist verboten, diesen Punkt zu überqueren* (forbidden to cross over this point.) By then, post-war Hungary had been taken over by the Soviet-Allied government and was part of the Eastern Bloc. The People's Republic of Hungary, created in 1949, lasted until the revolutions of 1989 when communism in Hungary ended. Being on my own I was quite fearful, and hastily retreated the way I had come, apprehensive that I might have unwittingly crossed the divide!

Another memorable occasion was when I was crossing the Dolomites into Italy. I had every intention of crossing the border and finding my accommodation before nightfall. I was bound for Trieste on the Italian/Yugoslavian border, where I planned to meet a colleague. To obtain petrol at a reduced price, visitors from outside the country were able to buy petrol coupons at the border. This I did, but as I was about to leave, I discovered to my dismay that I no longer had my wallet. I looked all around me to try and find it but eventually concluded that someone, probably a professional thief standing alongside me, must have stolen it. After much commotion and further searching I had no alternative than to accept the fact that it must have been stolen during that transaction. I was in quite a state because I literally had no money on me, not even to pay for my overnight accommodation. I had planned to visit a bank to draw out Italian lire. A stranger standing nearby was aware of my predicament and distress and offered to give me enough to cover my night's accommodation. I was overcome with gratitude to her. The following day I went through the procedure of contacting my insurance company and obtaining currency from a bank. Nothing seemed to daunt me at the time, as the above will have shown you.

Although flying made its debut shortly before WW1 it was not until the sixties that the passenger airline industry developed and flying became commonplace. Although I had learned to fly a Piper, I longed for the experience of an international passenger flight. Not telling my parents but only a few friends in France, I decided I would satisfy my longing and spend a short weekend in London.

It was with trepidation that I boarded my first passenger flight from Orly airport, Paris, not far from where I was living in Fontainebleau, to fly to London's Heathrow airport in 1960. I was slightly apprehensive that it might not make the take-off and I remember my relief when the plane lifted into the air and began flying smoothly high above the clouds When the plane began its descent as it flew across the English Channel, close to the French coast, I began to be fearful about its landing. What relief as it touched the runway and bumped along to a halt! My first commercial flight was safely over. I was certainly quite proud when I told my family and friends about it.

My travelogue includes flying to far-flung destinations, with those to Kenya, South Africa, Hong Kong, Canada, and Los Angeles being particularly memorable. Although flying now in the twenty-first century is commonplace, it is deleted from some people's agenda when they want to play their part in protecting the climate.

Little did I know at the time how my love of travel and my wanderings in those earlier years would shape my later career and permeate into the actual travelling public. I owe a lot to my husband, as if it weren't for him, my later life would have taken a different route.

CHAPTER 2

Pathway into Billington Travel

My last full-time post was at Rowena Girls' School in Sittingbourne, close to where my husband and I were living at the time in Faversham. I had overall responsibility for the lower school and was joint deputy head with the head of the upper school. My responsibilities included overseeing the 13-plus selection when around 15-20% of the girls were eligible to further their education in the local grammar school; this process was through general assessment and not by examination. The parents and guardians of each individual in that age group were invited for interview to discuss their daughter's suitability. Normally we came to the same conclusion, with only two or three appeals each year. Another responsibility was to visit local primary schools towards the end of the summer term in preparation for their transfer at the start of the new school year to our school.

I loved working in the school and the responsibilities involved as head of the lower school with my own office, getting to know the pupils and meeting regularly with their class teachers. There were times when a teacher might have difficulty in controlling a pupil's behaviour and then sent to me for the appropriate discipline. I recall one teacher who, constantly struggling to maintain discipline, absented herself without prior notice from work; it was not an easy situation to address and handle and to get to the roots. I was still teaching maths but only about 50% of the week, which was a good diversion and much enjoyed. I was truly happy and felt really fulfilled in all that this post at Rowena offered me.

It was quite a shock when after almost five years in the school, my life was interrupted and turned upside down by a diagnosis of breast cancer. It was not an easy passage to face; I first had an investigatory operation, which even my GP wasn't sure was necessary, passing the buck to me to make the decision as to whether I had an investigatory operation. After some deliberation I went ahead.

When back in the open ward following the operation, I was shocked to hear the news from my surgeon that he had needed to perform a mastectomy operation and that a course of radiotherapy would be required. All this took place in the autumn of 1978, coinciding with the early days of the Winter of Discontent, when there were widespread strikes by public sector trade unions, including nursing staff. I had been reassured when I was first admitted that this strike would have no effect on my care, so I didn't see this as an issue. It became obvious the following day when I was ordered to go on my own to take a bath, why none of the nursing or auxiliary staff seemed to care, seemingly having no understanding of the dread I had of seeing my 'mutilated' body.

My husband's caring nature came to the fore with his help and that of Mother and Mary, my sister, who immediately flew back from Riyadh in Saudi Arabia where she and her husband, Hugh—a quantity surveyor—were currently living. A month's radiotherapy in a somewhat archaic hospital near Rochester and I was well on my way to recovery. Friends rallied round to give me lifts to the hospital, two of whom, encouraging me along my journey of faith, suggested I attend a local church.

Looking back now on the whole episode I know I would have benefited enormously by some kind of talking therapy, but none was offered.

Although on extended sick leave at the time, in the circumstances I felt the best way forward, although it nearly broke my heart, was to give in my notice. I spent a couple of terms doing supply teaching in two schools close to our home in East Malling. It was the end of a career I loved and which I had been able to fulfil in my calling for almost 30 years. Many years later I took to tutoring youngsters of a variety of ages, most of whom lacked confidence (often in algebra), thus falling short of their true potential. It was great to see them start to gain confidence and flourish.

Once my teaching days were behind me, John and I were invited by a former colleague of John's to open and manage a new travel agency in the centre of Sevenoaks.

After a year's hard work, the newly found travel business proved to be a great success, giving us the encouragement to press on. However, it continued to give us a modest financial reward such that we made the decision to go it alone and open our own agency. After much property searching, we found suitable premises within a small but busy parade of shops in Riverhead just outside Sevenoaks where, in 1981, we opened Billington Travel. An adequate loan had first to be obtained and we were not able to start functioning properly for several months until we had been approved by the Association of British Travel Agents (ABTA).

I had been aware three years or so after we started the business that John was becoming less interested in it, leaving me to take control and only occasionally coming in to work himself during our actual opening hours and more often than not towards the end of the day. At the time, I put the situation down to depression, which he had suffered over a number of years. I was devastated when after three months so-called 'warning' he actually left me. He appeared to be excited in what he called a new venture, but under the surface I became aware that he was a bit apprehensive and unsure about the implications of what he was doing. Did he have a wee twinge of concern at leaving me? He did seek professional help but his mind was made up. So, to my consternation he went and I was left to face a different but nonetheless additional bereavement.

What John and I were able to share together over 15 years was Toby, our adorable, cuddly, black semi-Persian cat; he had been part of our lives since a kitten living with us and adapting to the various homes in which we had lived. (Yes, my former husband did have itchy feet!) Toby would be there to welcome us after work, sitting placidly on the wall or fence, but excitedly jumping down as soon as we appeared, with loud 'meows' of greeting. We loved and cared for him so much, perhaps taking the place of the children we never had.

I will never forget the comfort—yes, and empathy—Toby gave me the evening I returned from a day's work to read the note left on the kitchen table, saying John had left and would only return at some stage to collect his belongings which he'd left in the garage. From now on, I was to be on my own, deserted and bereaved, but not by Toby, who was my solace.

Such was the scene shortly before the Christmas of 1985. It had been many years since I had spent a night alone and I was quite fearful about the future and what it held for me. Toby sensed my distress and I recall how much I needed him to cuddle up to me and even allowed him to sleep on my bed at night. Little did I envisage that in a few months' time he would be no more, as he developed what proved to be a potentially fatal leukaemia. I put the cause of this down to his distress at losing John, for they were very close.

My family, who lived locally, were aware of what was happening but I was reluctant to talk about the effect these circumstances were having on me mentally, and on my emotions. It was not helped by the fact that this happened in December with Christmas just around the corner.

Christmas Day was spent with my family; I recall withdrawing from any meaningful conversation, sadly immersed in self-pity.

Epilogue

It was great that following our move to Sevenoaks John became a regular at the church I was attending, playing his part in helping with the bookstall, and finally professing his commitment through confirmation. I was saddened at the thought that he might well be distancing himself from the Christian faith. I didn't blame God for what was happening knowing that we are given free will. Now I see how these experiences were used for his purposes. My own faith was being sorely tested, but gradually over time it began to be my source of strength and God my anchor.

My grace is sufficient for you for my
strength is made perfect in weakness.
(2 Corinthians 12 v 9)

CHAPTER 3

Opening Doors of Billington Travel

I knew I had little alternative than to persevere, not just with life on my own at home, but with the responsibilities of the business now lying very heavily on my shoulders. The truth was that, like it or not, I was now the manager of Billington Travel and managing director of a limited company. How equipped was I to undertake all that was involved? Was this a situation in which I could draw on the experiences of the past and for which God had been preparing me? Ahead of me lay many responsibilities: the loan that, in due course, would have to be repaid, alongside staff salaries, rent, rates and all the other expenses one has in a small business. Not least was the responsibility of the core business, namely our clients' bookings and their holiday and travel plans. I had no option but to get on with the job and throw self-pity to the wind. I was much indebted to the staff I had at the time and was so grateful for their support of me personally, together with their constant reliability and efficiency.

Needing to put that crisis in the background, my future years were now to be focused on making a success of the business.

Others working in the world of small businesses would have said that Billington Travel didn't operate in a conventional way. That may well be true. My heartfelt desire was to create and offer a good, honest and personal touch to our clientele, who were entrusting us with their travel needs. For me this was more important than making high profits. I expected the staff I employed to adopt a service equal to my own. Travel agencies such as ours have not been frontrunners in the world of profit making. In the circumstances, the remuneration I received was sufficient for a relatively good standard of living, and sufficient to meet the practical needs and expenses of the business as well as my own everyday needs.

As an independent travel agency, we were much aware of being in competition with the multiples. However, we prided ourselves on the time and personal touch we offered and spent on our clients. This customer service was much valued and our clients would return with their travel needs on a regular basis.

Those living in the Riverhead area seemed pleased that a travel agency such as ours that gave the delicate touch was so near at hand and they began to drift in to find out first hand for themselves. We soon started to recognise their faces, greeting them by name when they came through our doors and even as we passed them in the street.

The greatest 'ups' for us were the encouraging messages from clients who called or phoned to tell us that their holiday, that we had arranged for them, had gone according to plan and that they had had an enjoyable time. We were also delighted to win over the years a variety of travel agency awards.

As a travel agent we were privileged to have the opportunity in 1987 to visit London City Airport before it was officially opened and then in the spring of 1994 to have a flavour of experiencing a journey through the Channel Tunnel at the time of its opening.

When free educational trips to a variety of destinations across the globe came our way, I was keen for a member of our staff to go. Each had to understand that they were not occasions just to have a good time but were with the aim that the business as a whole would benefit from what they would experience and learn. I elected to go on those offered by the French government tourist office to gain experience of areas of France with which I was unfamiliar.

We held Billington Travel open evenings several times a year meeting just across the road at the village hall; there would always be refreshments; a carefully selected person would be invited to give a talk about a particular topic or destination, and I would give details of a pending tour. Unless the weather was unfavourable, these open evenings were well attended and enjoyed. To have been able to work our way onto the map and increase our clientele was gratifying. Being aware of the diverse types of service that other agencies in the town were offering, we knew it was the personal touch and satisfaction we gave that won the day! I would frequently remind the staff of this, telling them that my own aim for the business was to give this service and for it not necessarily to be a money spinner. However, it was very encouraging when we *did* make a financially profitable booking!

In the early years of Billington Travel, bookings would be settled by cheque or with cash. If a client we didn't know wanted to pay by cheque, we would need to ask the client to go to the local bank for cash; to our minds this was no great problem as each of five main banks had a branch close by in Riverhead. There were those people who felt affronted by that request and would stalk out never to be seen again. Money was at stake, and we stood our ground. We occasionally did have a bounced cheque.

As a staff we had gradually to adapt to the digital age as computers and credit cards came into use. Even phones changed and we became frustrated when we had to press one digit after another to get through to a particular person or department only to be cut off! We were aware that in those early days we were ahead of the public on our computers with the ability to make our bookings online and accounting systems changed. This was a learning curve for us all but we did make a point of attending appropriate training courses and sessions that were offered to travel agents, some of them thankfully 'in-house'.

There was one particular situation I found difficult to handle when at the close of a service in church I might be greeted with words such as, 'I am so glad I have found you—sorry to bother you—but as I am planning to go to Cyprus next month and I wondered whether you could recommend some three-star hotels in Cyprus and also the best airline to use?' It was encouraging and re-assuring that an increasing number of the congregation would want to book with us. However, I saw Sunday as my day off!

We were certainly not without our 'downs' over those years. One of the downs took place on Thursday, 15 October 1987. I was one of the few who slept through that night. On Friday morning I awoke to the mystery of having no electricity and to total silence due to the absence of traffic outside. I thought the end of the world had come! When I eventually ventured to explore what was happening, everywhere I looked I saw fallen trees, damaged roofs, fences completely flattened and much else. Fortunately, my own house and our office building were undamaged.

Sevenoaks had been the epicentre of the hurricane. Six of the renowned seven Coronation Oaks at the edge of the historic Vine Cricket Ground, as well as countless trees in Knole Park, were flattened—all this by winds of over 100mph. With no electricity for nearly a week and roads blocked and closed, we had no option but to close our doors until some normality was restored.

Another 'down' was being awakened by police in the night to be informed that the office premises had been broken into and 'could I go down immediately'. I recall shaking as I dressed and rushed to the scene to liaise with the police, assess the damage done and identify what had been stolen. I then had to deal with broken doors and front windows and ensure that they were boarded up. This scenario happened more than once!

Cash and tickets were kept in the safe, so when the burglar could not find anything valuable to steal, he would invariably give vent to his frustration by throwing papers, files and brochures everywhere. I think I bore most of these occasions with a modicum of resilience!

Entrusted with the travel requirements of members of the public on a daily basis, there were inevitably a number of occasions when we fell victim to errors on the part of tour operators. Sadly, these could not always be rectified. Then there were occasions when insurance companies would wriggle out of the terms of their policies even when the client's claim was genuine. I pride myself that I was usually successful in resolving these with the insurers in the end.

A highlight for me were the group travel tours I organised over the years to France and to many Biblical lands. These trips spanned 30 years with the final one to Rome taking place in 2019 (long after I had sold the business in 2005). Working with an affiliated tour operator to give us financial protection was essential. Publicity for each tour was key: I would write and put together a small brochure outlining the proposed itinerary and full details. As soon as I had sufficient bookings to make it financially viable, these bookings would be passed on to the travel company operator.

I still have a small brochure of special interest holidays offered by Billington Travel from 1997. Let me give a flavour of what we offered in those early days. There was an escorted tour to Paris on which I have a clear recollection of ending up one evening after dinner in the 'red light' district by mistake! Another was 'Off the Beaten Track in Israel' which I led with the Revd Dr Roger Curl, a former minister of my church, and a third one was a nine-day family Christian holiday to Houlgate on the north coast of Normandy, which I organised for our church with Roger as the chaplain guest speaker. No coach for this one, for we went in our own cars, giving lifts to those who, for whatever reason, were unable to drive there. Having lived in France for five years I knew the country well and loved the opportunities these tours gave to return to that country and share its delights with others.

In 1998 I was diagnosed yet again with breast cancer, requiring a similar operation to the one I'd had previously, but this time it was to be followed up with specified medication prescribed to be taken for four years and not radiotherapy. I needed to be open about having the operation but found it easier just to disclose its nature to family and close friends. I recovered so well and quickly that, only five weeks later, I was able to lead one of our tours to the Holy Land as planned.

For the purposes of this book, I have collected contributions from those with whom I co-led the groups, namely our chaplains-cum-tour-leaders. Others are from some of the recipients themselves, giving readers a tempting glimpse and insight of our experiences.

I continued to owe much to three core members of our staff, on whom I could depend. This meant that I, who was always known for my busyness in life, could devote sufficient time to the organisation and promotion of the tours. Many of the earlier tours we offered were to northern France travelling by coach: Burgundy with its champagne cellars, the Chateaux of the Loire, the Seine Valley staying in Giverny in order to visit Monet's gardens, the gardens of northern France and last but not least to Fontainebleau, where I had lived for five years. Then there were also not to be forgotten the countless day trips across the Channel mostly to Boulogne where clients after a typical 'prix fixe' lunch would avail themselves of duty-frees!

In 2004 I considered the time was ripe to sell the business. Strangely, it was the personal touch we offered our clients that proved a sticking point in negotiations. Even my own honesty and integrity was queried. For me, the whole stressful process of selling the business was a marathon— so vastly different from selling a house—but eventually in 2005 Billington Travel, name and all, was sold. It has in these intervening years passed ownership to another and is in good hands. Long may that continue!

Earlier this year I met with four of our former staff for lunch. I have subsequently asked each of them to write a brief contribution of their memories whilst working with Billington Travel.

Billington Travel in Riverhead

Anthea Parkin writes: *It was early 1986 and I'd been invited for an interview at Billington Travel. With a son settled at primary school and a daughter nearing her first birthday, I felt ready to step back into the workplace. So, at 2 o'clock that Wednesday afternoon, in response to a newspaper advertisement asking for accounting assistance a few hours a week, I found myself outside the Riverhead travel agency. The door was firmly shut and showing CLOSED and it seemed no-one was inside. This should have puzzled me but of course in those days it was normal for village shops and small businesses to close for half a day midweek. There was a slight niggle though as I knocked again that perhaps the owner had forgotten the appointment when suddenly, as if out of nowhere (the back office), Wendy Billington emerged. When the door was opened I little realised what a journey I was about to embark on, and one that would last 18 years!*

Once installed in the tiny back office that I shared with Wendy's secretary (she did mornings, I did afternoons) I was able to take over the routine day-to-day accountancy tasks. My four hours a week soon grew as I became more involved in the business and became aware of the ins and outs of the travel industry. However, it was early on during a visit to Paris with Wendy—a day trip to arrange a new bank account to facilitate the running of Billington's French breakaway holidays—that I got to know and understand the real Wendy. As I learned about her background, her very different previous career, how she had found herself faced with the challenge of running for the first time her own business, I knew I wanted to be part of the team that was to reinvent Billington Travel.

From its humble premises a unique travel business grew. It was unique in many ways, with its travel evenings, Wendy belonging to a business breakfast group, all the while taking pride in the attention to detail and personal expertise and care given to every booking. Most important though was the fact that the staff worked as a team and enjoyed the friendship that came with it. We were allowed to share and implement our ideas and to enjoy educational visits. Alongside my financial role I was happy to help with marketing, in which I had some experience. We adapted to new trends and became cruise specialists in a field that was growing rapidly. One area following in the footsteps of Wendy and very dear to my heart was the opportunity I had to lead with my husband our own specialist guided tours to places we loved. Barcelona, a favourite city, was enjoyed by clients, as were the Dutch bulb fields. Wendy meantime was leading her own tours to many places including her much loved France, and they were proving popular. The local community were able to enjoy theatre visits too and even a day at the races courtesy of their local travel agency.

Going past Billington Travel today can trigger a lump in my throat, but it's good to see that the name lives on alongside my own personal memories. I was happy to be part of its journey for all those years.

Shenda writes: *I learned so much about France, in particular northern France, Pas de Calais, Normandy and Paris. Billington Travel ran a small tour operation to these regions. We were lucky enough to all be taken to a chateau for an overnight stay in Chantilly, a town famous for its lace. We also travelled to Paris by Eurostar to view hotels that were featured in the tour operation. Very memorable and fun times were had by all! Thanks to Wendy.*

Anne Fielder writes: *Returning to travel after a 10-year break was a wish come true. I much enjoyed working with Wendy and at different periods of my time at Billington Travel with Graham, Hillary, Jackie, Donna, Shenda, Gary and Min, serving our lovely clients who came back time and time again. I had too a chance to travel, all this making my 13 years at Billington Travel fly by.*

Sandra writes: *After a long gap of not working in travel and living abroad, Wendy gave me the opportunity in 1997 to start again and work for her at Billington Travel. I really enjoyed my time there, learning new things and making very good friends.*

CHAPTER 4

Glimpses into Counselling

First Steps

It is now 40 years since I had an opportunity to train as a bereavement counsellor, but I haven't forgotten the salient points of that course. In those four intervening decades, I have seen the way that counselling has evolved from its infancy, when it was almost taboo to admit to being on its receiving end. Now with mental health issues on the increase most people acknowledge the value of this talking therapy, knowing that it can make a profound impact on individuals, families and even communities as they navigate difficult life situations. Listening is at its key, guiding the speaker towards finding ways to resolve for themselves the particular issues that are troubling them and affecting their everyday lives.

In the mid-eighties, Reverend Tony Groom—the newly appointed first head of Sevenoaks Counselling Service and member with his family of our church congregation— encouraged me to train as a bereavement counsellor. At first, I was daunted by the prospect; it was certainly an encouragement that he saw me as suitable material for this particular ministry. 'Nothing ventured, nothing gained' as the saying goes! I took a leap, applied to do the evening course in London and was accepted. Looking back, I can see now that this was God's path for me. These were my first steps into the pastoral world for which I knew I had both an interest and heart.

Soon after qualifying, my first referral and client was a lady in her late thirties. I counselled her before and after the death of one of her parents. She would drive from London to my home in Sevenoaks and we would sit together in the living room as she shared and I listened to her sad journey of loss. Through my own experiences of bereavement, including that of my beloved soulmate and of my Father, I slipped subconsciously into the role of an empathetic listener. She did become dependent on me during the earlier sessions. When I saw that she was able to stand on her own two feet and take up life again I worked towards ending these times together.

Sevenoaks Counselling Service

Sevenoaks Christian Counselling Service, as it was originally called, was founded in 1982 and has now just celebrated its fortieth anniversary. Over the decades it has touched and changed the lives of countless clients.

Although not actively involved in its early years, I attended the same church as one of the original trustees, whose wife played a major role in its beginnings. As a member of a pastoral care team, those struggling with their marriages would come to her for help and advice. She longed to be able to help but gradually became aware that, although she was prepared to listen to distressing situations, it was beyond her capabilities to help in any practical way. She was out of her depth. To whom could she turn? She decided to talk it through with the rector, the Reverend Kenneth Prior.

It was such a relief for her to be able to offload and acknowledge that this particular situation, as well as others she had come across in the course of her pastoral work, were beyond her limitations. He listened to her with genuine concern and understanding and prayed for God's help and guidance for the way forward. She went away not just with that sense of relief but one of expectation. With Kenneth himself leading the way, the vision of a counselling service within Sevenoaks began to take shape and root.

Sevenoaks Christian Counselling Service was registered as a limited company and recognised by the charity commission. Tony Groom became the head of counselling, moving with his family and precious cat from Dundee, where he was chaplain of Nine Elms Hospital, to a new life in Sevenoaks. He had a wealth of pastoral experience to offer with a wide knowledge of psychology and counselling itself. With the decision made and thanks to the generosity of a number of people who shared the vision, sufficient funds were soon in place to make it all possible and the counselling service was born. During those early years the SCCS owed much to the thoughtfulness and kindness of St Nicholas Church, who provided rooms and facilities in their church hall without charge. After those first few years more permanent premises were offered by the United Reform Church located near Sevenoaks Station.

Reflecting now on its beginnings, I am aware that this whole enterprise was an act of faith, guided by God and an answer to the prayers of many. As a trustee I have been actively involved within the service over many years, retiring at the end of 2021. The way it has evolved over four decades into the thriving service that it now is has been amazing and beyond my wildest dreams! Thousands of lives have been changed by the faithful service of its highly qualified and experienced counsellors (currently numbering 14). It owes much to them and to two of its former heads of counselling—Tony Groom and Maureen King—each of whom served so faithfully over many years and also to Sue Surgeanor, who is the current head of counselling today. Steering the ship have been the chairpersons, the longest serving one being Stephen Scott. Regular prayer breakfasts, newsletters and annual open meetings have taken place over the years. I can recall attending prayer meetings with fellow trustees which took place before work at 7am. I was normally the only female! Much is owed to those who have supported the service through prayer and financial support including local churches and grants from local bodies.

I was flattered and encouraged that my work had not been in vain when, following my retirement, Maureen King, a former head of counselling wrote a tribute to me in the counselling newsletter, of which I will give you a snippet:

'*The little lady with a big heart whose loyalty, hospitality, readiness to offer help when a task needed doing, her vision for counselling well before it became trendy, and her support to the counsellors and volunteers is second to none. Because of her life experiences and training in people helping, Wendy is very committed to helping people who are experiencing pain and problems in their lives*'.

What an experience, learning curve and privilege it has been for me to serve as a trustee all those years! The service and all that it stands for will always remain dear to my heart.

In the prophecy of Isaiah there is reference to Jesus as 'Wonderful Counsellor', so vividly demonstrated throughout his earthly life, listening, giving of his time in his four years of ministry and responding to the needy who crossed his path.

We are reminded in Psalm 23 of the assurance of God's protective hand as he our shepherd guides us his sheep into fresh and green pastures and beside still waters. This beautiful psalm of David, known to many across the globe, I would commend us all to read, learn and to absorb into our hearts in meaningful ways.

The LORD is my shepherd, I lack nothing.
He makes me lie down in green pastures,
he leads me beside quiet waters,
he refreshes my soul.
He guides me along the right paths for his name's sake.

Even though I walk through the darkest valley,
I will fear no evil,
for you are with me; your rod and your staff,
they comfort me.
You prepare a table before me in the presence of my
enemies. You anoint my head with oil; my cup overflows.
Surely your goodness and love will follow me all the days
of my life, and I will dwell in the house of the Lord forever.
(Psalm 23)

CHAPTER 5

Call to Pastoral Ministry

'The word pastoral conjures up for me a picture of a shepherd gathering together his wandering flock of sheep on a hillside above the Sea of Galilee—lovingly tending, leading, protecting, and nurturing them.' These are the first words of the introduction to the book I wrote in 2010, *Growing a Caring Church*, written during the period when I was a pastoral assistant in my church; glancing at the contents of the book now I see that they are just as relevant today as they were when I wrote it 12 years ago.

Training for Pastoral Ministry

As a consequence of earlier experiences in my life and alongside identifying myself as a 'people person', I felt that God was calling me into pastoral ministry. Still immersed in the busy life of running Billington Travel, I researched a variety of courses and finally decided on one on pastoral care held in the evenings at Spurgeon's College, a decision I will never regret; it gave me confidence that I was well-trained and equipped to serve as a pastoral assistant within my parish church in Sevenoaks. I had been invited by our Rector, Reverend Miles Thomson, to serve as pastoral assistant in a voluntary capacity in our church. I accepted and was commissioned by the Rector and church wardens during a church service. At the time it was all a bit awesome for me. Although I had been trained at Spurgeon's College and also by the diocese, I wondered whether it would all be too much for me to undertake. Deep down I did believe that it was in line with God's will for me to serve him in this way. In those early years when I still owned and manged the business, I employed a new member of staff and gave a promotion to another, enabling my time to be split between the two.

Early Years

I liaised with and was graciously supported by each of our two successive Rectors; gradually I was given more opportunity and responsibility to oversee many of the pastoral needs within our church family. A diversity of these slowly became apparent as they began to cross my path or were referred to me. If they were of a spiritual nature and if appropriate, I would refer to our Rector, who I would meet on a regular basis.

A shared pastoral ministry was of the essence, and it was encouraging to bring together volunteers each equipped with and ready to share their individual skills for the benefit of fellow Christians.

In this new role as pastoral assistant, it was apparent that I needed first to categorise and assess the issues and draw in others with pastoral hearts, time and skills to assist.

Bereavement

I was aware of a few who were grieving following the loss of a loved one and in some cases lapsing into depression. When the need for professional help was apparent, I would encourage an appointment with their GP. If they were reluctant to do so I would ask sensitively if they would like me to accompany them and, in some cases, they were more than willing for me to do so. As a bereavement counsellor myself I was able to offer support, either on a one-to-one basis or through small bereavement support groups that I set up and led over many years.

Relationship Concerns

These tended to be hidden and it was only when a person was reassured of confidentiality that they might seek a listening ear and help. Having suffered a broken marriage myself, I am acutely aware of both the preciousness and the fragility of a marriage relationship. Not long after I became involved in pastoral work, we were able to offer to our church community a Marriage Enrichment Course originating from Holy Trinity Brompton Church in London, which has now helped countless couples across the globe over the years. When it was suitable for the couple, I would suggest that they consider attending this course.

Financial Issues

There were those struggling financially. Within our church there still is a Fellowship Fund into which any church member can contribute. It is run by a small committee who are totally confidential. They assess a person's financial circumstances and, in some cases, arrange a loan or gift. A local debt bureau is another source of help.

Listening

A vital key to pastoral work and to our everyday lives as a whole. I had attended a week's listening course with 'Acorn Listeners', so I was able to offer listening courses on a regular basis, drawing together a small group of no more than 12, normally for seven sessions. Here they learned early in the course that good listening is more than just words, but also the way these are expressed in body language and facial expressions.

Befrienders

This is an organisation that has operated within our local community for over 17 years. Its aim is to befriend those who are finding life difficult to manage and need an understanding person who could befriend them and have the opportunity to chat about things that were going on in their everyday lives. They are referred by professionals such as social services or medical practitioners. Each befriender agrees to visit an individual on a regular basis for a few months once a week or a fortnight. Here again, good listening heads the list of the skills needed and I still am available to play a role in the short training that each befriender receives.

Visiting

For individuals and families, the value it carries is not to be underestimated. I soon found that the need was more than

I could personally handle. As a consequence, I gradually drew together a handful of deeply committed Christians, who had a passion to use their 'people-centred' gifts in their service for God and for the benefit of others. I would call on them as and when required.

We needed to be alert to those who were housebound—the elderly and those feeling alone or lonely, not forgetting church members in nursing and residential care homes. Thus, further individuals with empathetic qualities were approached and invited to visit those who had over the years been regular attenders of the church.

These different visiting groups would meet together to discuss particular issues that crossed our paths and on a regular basis to pray. They were given a brief training in listening skills to learn how essential it was to draw up boundaries of time with each person they were visiting, but these were not always easy to keep!

Lifts

Lifts to church services and hospital and medical appointments during the week were on our agenda. For the latter we created a small group of retired people—mostly men—who gave of their time with such commitment, generosity of time and dedication. Unfortunately, we did not have sufficient volunteers to meet the need for church lifts on Sundays, but we did our best!

Delivery of meals

These proved to be a treat for anyone! It was certainly a welcome token of care for those who had recently been discharged from hospital, were unwell or maybe just wanting to be cheered up. We were fortunate to have a very willing band of volunteers to cook and deliver what would often be the main meal of the day.

Marriage and Marriage Preparation Courses

These are still offered within our church today. Now that they are on Zoom, they have attracted couples from the wider community. Alan and Margaret are an ideal couple to write about the history of these courses, which I have therefore invited them to do. This contribution can be found in the Addendum.

Dementia

Despite my own busy school schedule, I saw the need to enhance my own ministry through specific training courses. One of immense value was the dementia support programme offered and run by Pilgrim Homes—a nationwide charity for the elderly. This training course was held in London on five successive Saturdays, with a former trained lecturer on dementia, who herself had developed the condition, giving one of the lectures on her personal first-hand insights into dementia. She subsequently started to write a book focused on her own journey through dementia, completed by another when her condition deteriorated.

Suicide Prevention

Another important course of enormous value, the details of which I remember to this day, was on 'Suicide Prevention', offered by our local social services.

Mentoring Others in Training

I was invited to become a mentor to others who were following a diocesan training course to become pastoral assistants, which I did over a number of years. The bonus was being able to get to know individuals from other churches.

Pastoral Supervision

The regular pastoral supervision I received throughout my ministry was something I treasured. I was able to share day-to-day concerns confidentially with a highly experienced pastoral counsellor and clergyman who was not associated directly with my church. I greatly appreciated this person as he accompanied me on my own spiritual journey of faith.

Moving On

Five years on since I officially retired from this pastoral ministry I was recognised by being given the honourable title of Pastoral Assistant Emeritus by the Rochester Diocese. Looking back now, I realise the ways God had prepared and equipped me for this ministry to which I had been called. On a number of occasions, I felt weak and inadequate, but throughout those years I was aware of God's constant helping and guiding hand as I sought to show his love to others.

To have been part of this pastoral ministry has been for me an enormous privilege and I trust that in a variety of ways God has used me to touch the lives of others for his purposes. All our experiences of life are a learning curve, becoming a positive tool for the future.

Alongside the changes that have been made in our church recently, the pastoral ministry is a shared one with overall responsibility passed on into the capable hands of each of the pastors of our four congregations. Jesus in the most beautiful and challenging words in John's gospel compares us, his followers, as the branches joined to himself, the vine.

> *I am the vine; you are the branches.*
> *If a man remains in me and I in him,*
> *he will bear much fruit;*
> *apart from me you can do nothing. (John 15 v 5)*

CHAPTER 6

Pandemic Experiences

At the start of this book, I mentioned that there had been two global episodes of major significance, each of which has adversely affected the everyday lives of countless people. One was the experience of WW2, which had a profound effect overall on my mental and emotional equilibrium, not least through my disrupted education. The other was the catastrophic pandemic. From the start I was determined not to allow it to get the better of me.

Following our Rome tour in 2019 I had a longing to go just once more to the Holy Land and at the same time to give the opportunity to others perhaps for the first time to experience all that the country had to offer. The itinerary was in place for April 2020, bookings made and excitement in the air. Then Covid struck. I am an optimist, holding out as long as I could before the monies paid were in jeopardy. I finally had to capitulate and make the decision that we just had to cancel the tour. Within the UK at the time Covid-19 cases were on the increase, restrictions as to how we led our everyday lives were in place and we were in 'lockdown'.

On Day 1 of lockdown outdoor exercise was restricted and permitted for just once a day. I was determined to go out each morning and aided by my stick take a walk in Knole Park close to where I lived. It's a park renowned both for its historic house built in the sixteenth century and its deer. I found a bench seat on which to sit not far down the steep slope close to the entrance. The only folk I met then were the sprinters out for their daily exercises; occasionally one of them would stop for a brief friendly chat. I found that almost all would greet me as they passed. Apart from dog walkers there were hardly any others who ventured out. This proved to be for me a great opportunity to have fresh air, to slow down and be able to watch the first signs of spring and as I did to meditate on God's wonderful creation. It was as if I were in another world—so peaceful and those who passed me so friendly. God seemed very close.

When allowed during lockdown I would invite friends to visit me and we sat together just a short distance from one other on my small back patio. They would come armed with their own drink and each wearing a mask. Churches had to close, as did most shops with the exception of those selling essential foods. I chose to order online with a delivery once a fortnight.

I did all I could to prevent myself from catching the virus; washing my hands frequently, wearing my mask whenever others were in close proximity and ensuring that the house was well ventilated were all of high priority. It was a virus that spread rapidly and seemed to be spiralling out of control. Hospitals were overflowing and nurses and other medics were at breaking point; however ill a person became, family and friends were forbidden to visit, even when death was said to be imminent. Amongst these were residents I knew well in a nearby residential home, where I had over a number of years taken Sunday morning services, and now I was unable to say *au revoir*.

The red-letter day came on 4 January 2021, and the first people received the Oxford University/AstraZeneca coronavirus vaccination; so much credit goes to the scientists who worked against all the odds to create it. When it became available to older people like me, we would queue up in an orderly fashion at special designated centres. I have every admiration for the way this was organised and administered. It would normally become effective after three weeks and only after a further three jabs could we relax, knowing that even if we caught the virus the consequences were diminished. Sadly, now three years on I am acutely aware of those who are currently still suffering from 'long Covid'. My heart goes out to the many grieving the loss of loved ones.

I recall the restrictions, fears, disrupted life and education that were experienced during the war years due to a measure which can be compared with those of the pandemic, when we were no longer in control of our everyday lives.

It was in September 2020 during the first year of the pandemic that my dear sister, Mary, passed away just two years after her husband, Hugh, died in a nearby hospice. It was a peaceful end and not unexpected, and in her own home close to where I lived—looked after by a 'live-in' carer.

The reality of her death and loss hit me hard a few months later. Not having children, I felt so alone. Hospice in the

Weald came to my rescue and were able to offer me a number of counselling sessions, not 'face to face' as this was prohibited, but on Zoom. I found this so therapeutic to be able to offload all that was troubling me and to have a listener with such empathy and understanding. My loss went deep but gradually I have been able to weave it into my life, accepting it in a realistic way. I felt free and able to talk about my Christian faith as well as that of Mary's South African carer, who shortly before Mary died talked about how freely she was able to share her own testimony with Mary. This caught me by surprise as Mary throughout her life was unable to take part in any discussions connected with Christianity, often having to leave the room to avoid them. It was a surreal moment as I listened open-mouthed to the carer, as she spoke about Mary having made a confession of faith shortly before she passed away based on her desire to join Hugh in heaven. He himself had become a Christian earlier in his life. For me I believe the lives of us all are in God's hands. I will not know this side of heaven the depth of understanding of her commitment. Although the pandemic restricted the number of those who could be invited to her cremation service, to those who attended, it proved to be a particularly special one of thanksgiving for her 93 years of life.

The aftermath of the pandemic still sees a few individuals succumbing to the virus, but fortunately with fewer symptoms and cases declining. Not to be forgotten are those who are still suffering from long Covid. It has also seen long-term effects across the whole of our country's economy, seriously affecting the financial situation and standard of living within many lives.

The time is ripe for me to write one more chapter, exploring my current thoughts on what it is that keeps me going on my own particular journey.

My times are in your hands. (Psalm 31 v15)

CHAPTER 7

Living in the Here and Now

Just as the different reaches of a flowing river are an integral part of the river, so are our latter years an integral part of life itself.

That final reach of a river towards its estuary is sometimes known to be one of the most productive. Now that I am in part of the final stage of life it is appropriate that I explore channels where I can be productive as I seek to serve those who cross my path. As a Christian journeying through this last stage of life, I believe God requires me to be his tool for what may be the delicate work he has for me to do. In helping others, I can share the joys and peace it brings me as his follower, praying he will give me the strength and determination to do so. With the pandemic virtually behind us we are now able to return to the freedom of coming and going at will. One thing I need to learn to accept is that I can no longer live my life as I did prior to the pandemic with the need to move into the slow lane. For example, my regular trips to visit the homeless in the Waterloo Centre in London have had to be abandoned.

As I start to evaluate my limitations, I become acutely aware that I have much for which to be thankful. First of all—where I live. I made a wise move over 12 years ago to move from Shoreham—a delightful country riverside village on the Kent North Downs—to a cottage in the centre of Sevenoaks; it is near the parish church where I worship and to which I can still walk, close to the shops and to the beautiful grounds of Knole Park. My home is in a peaceful setting a few metres down a driveway—away from the noise of traffic. I couldn't wish for a better location. I am thankful that I still have a relatively active mind, enjoy good health and am able to offer hospitality welcoming friends into my home for coffee or a light meal. Karen—a delightful person with whom I relate well—comes on a weekly basis to clean my house. All this is so positive.

To add a further positivity to my list is that, to my relief, my former husband is living a contented life with his partner. He and I are in regular contact, meeting at least once a year in a local family country club to which I belong. Our time together is for each of us very therapeutic, playing a vital role in the reconciliation process, able to be open with each other and converse on quite a deep level.

On the negative side are my 'pancaked' feet, deformed toes and a fused ankle with consequentially poor balance that are my downfall! Eager not to be defeated and knowing that exercise is essential, I now use a stick for short distances and a four-wheel lightweight rollator for longer ones, enabling me to do my own shopping—no longer dependent on deliveries. I endeavour to keep to my own discipline of a twenty-minute daily walk. There are occasions that I need to use a taxi. When the taxi driver is late memories of the past come floating back of the luxury of having a chauffeur at one's beck and call, as Uncle Jim did back in 1939. On a more realistic note, weighing the positives with the negatives of the current stage of my life, it is obvious that the positives win.

In my latter years from time to time I catch myself pondering on what it is that keeps me going. High on the list are my friends – married couples and those who are single or widowed. No two relationships are the same, each of which helps to bring purpose into my life and are valued. It is true to say that all are younger than I am. Each of us is not without troubles and anxieties but with mutual understanding, empathy and listening ear we can pray for and encourage one another along life's way.

Having recently lost both Mary, my sister, and Hugh, her husband, my remaining family consists of their two sons, my nephews, and their offspring. They're there in the background of my life, 'on call' as it were, each playing an important role in encouraging me to keep going, as does my former husband.

My Christian faith without doubt is as central to my life as it has ever been. It has deepened and blossomed over the years, growing from that tiny mustard seed (suffice it to say not always well nourished!) into a deep-rooted plant. God is my anchor and so real to me in my everyday life. I am so conscious of his love for me and mine for him—my friend and my joy and, through his Spirit, a part of me.

The Bible has come alive in a very deep way as it did for many other fellow pilgrims on our escorted tours to the

Holy Land. We visited Golgotha, known as the authentic site of Jesus's crucifixion, and the Garden Tomb, not claiming to be the actual burial site of Jesus, but with similarities as described in the Bible—each located just outside the city walls of old Jerusalem. Then northward to the peace and beauty of the lake and hills of Galilee where, following the resurrection, he appears to his disciples beside the lake. Following in the footsteps of Jesus on these tours to the Holy Land has been like putting a jigsaw together. Any doubts of the total authenticity of the Bible, including what we read in the Gospels of Jesus' earthly ending with his death, resurrection and ascension have flown out of the window, reinforced by the reality of the living Lord's presence within my life now.

My deep Christian faith in God and my human relationships are what keep me going, giving me that longing not to give up but to press on. Paul uses the analogy of a race, constantly striving toward our goal. As a runner starts out on the course not carrying any unnecessary baggage so I hand over all the concerns and problems of my current life to God himself.

The message from the parable of the Good Samaritan I see primarily as voluntarily rendering help to another in distress, although being under no obligation to do so. Like many others we meet in the day to day of life, the least I can do in this last stage of my earthly life is to try to follow in the Samaritan's footsteps and offer a helping hand whenever it is needed.

The joys and sorrows I have experienced within my river of life have led me now to its estuary. I am still pressing on, protected, nourished and valuing the here and now towards the ultimate goal and hope of eternal life.

This is the day that the Lord has made.
Let us rejoice and be glad in it. (Psalm 118 v 18)

St Nicholas Church Sevenoaks

ADDENDUM

Marriage Ministry

Alan and Margaret Bowen write:

The Marriage Course originated from Holy Trinity Brompton Church (HTB) in West London 18 years ago. When one of our ministers asked if we were interested in running a similar one in our church, we responded positively.

Our Rector and his wife started by creating Bible teaching evenings on marriage at which, with the help of our pastoral assistant Wendy Billington, Margaret and I assisted.

The suggestion then was made that the three of us might value a day conference being offered at HTB. The conference's purpose was to show representatives from churches around the UK how they could run both a Marriage Course (for married couples) and a Marriage Preparation Course (for engaged couples). Attending this conference put us on fire with enthusiasm to run both courses in Sevenoaks! Wendy in particular greatly encouraged us to start all the necessary planning straightaway!

We warmed to the material of both courses written and developed by the Reverend Nicky and Sila Lee and the amazing way in which they presented it. Initially created just for their own church, they then decided 'to tee up all the resources' so they could be used by others in their own churches. The Marriage Course was aimed at all couples—not just those who might be struggling in their relationship.

In those early days we played an audio cassette; each couple had their own guest manual and every now and again the cassette was paused to allow each couple to have a private conversation based on that evening's theme. Essentially the course allowed each couple to talk privately about issues in a protected environment, which they probably would never 'get round to talking about' otherwise!

The course video was shown on a large screen viewed by the couples from their own tables. Classical music was softly played during conversation times so that everything they said to each other remained entirely private. In the process we recruited a wonderful Marriage Course team of helpers who did the cooking, setting up and decorating etc. at each session. Our team even went on fun weekends together to France to bond and enjoy our deepening friendships!

After a while we decided to change and do the speaking ourselves with the three of us participating at each course session—Alan and Margaret as the 'married couple' and Wendy speaking as someone who knew the pain of divorce and who had a passion to help others to maintain strong marriages. Wendy's involvement in the Sevenoaks Counselling Service also enabled her, as appropriate, to suggest to couples whose relationship struggles had reached potential breaking point to seek 'professional' counselling on a one-to-one basis.

We were eager to create a welcoming and warm atmosphere: flowers on each couple's tables and a two-course meal lovingly cooked and served by our team of dedicated volunteers.

In developing the course materials, Nicky and Sila subsequently created a highly professional video resource for each of the two courses. In recent years these videos have been updated and now also address all the 'modern' relationship issues caused by mobile phones and social media etc. The videos are a superb and highly relevant resource!

As we look back now on these last 18 years it has been a huge privilege to have been able help enrich the marriages of so many couples, as well as to build the foundations of engaged couples at the start of their marriage journey.

Wendy's personal enthusiasm and backing for both these courses was huge and with her constant encouragement we ourselves developed such a strong passion to use the wonderful resources, that we continue to be very active right up to the present time. Since 2014 we have run 18 marriage courses in St Nicholas and we've lost count of the number of engaged couples who have completed marriage preparation! Thank you, Wendy, for all you have done to support this endeavour over many years!

Wendy's 90th birthday

Special friends Helen Jack and George Crusher

Wendy with Angela Kent and Rosemary Cranfield

Wendy with Angela Kent and Margaret Bowen

Marriage Course Team

Escorted Tours 1990–2019

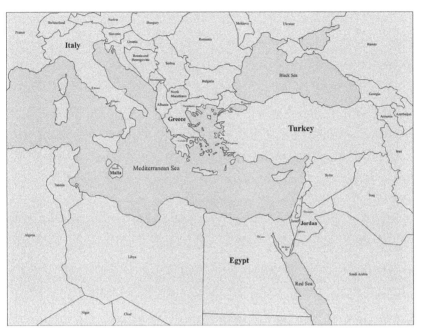

To add a bit of spice to the many tours I have organised and led over the years, I have invited a few of our pilgrims to make short contributions of their memories of one of the countries they visited, with the co-leaders being asked to write longer ones. Each contributor has their own style and way of writing and I have thus included these verbatim. Some of those from co-leaders have made a point of weaving in their own unique style of humour, and even if I thought about précising these, I know I wouldn't get it right and it might even be seen as sacrilege to do so!

For me it was a privilege to have been organiser and at the helm of tours to the Middle East supported by co-leaders. The Reverend Dr Roger Curl, Vicar of Mary's Church Kensington, was co-leader and chaplain to most of these. His extensive knowledge of the Bible, Hebrew and New Testament Greek, together with his clarity of mind and gift of delivery and subtle sense of humour, played such a valuable part. He is renowned for his excellent preaching. I recall when visiting his church, I and others alike would rarely leave without having learned a spiritual truth through his sermon (normally just 20 minutes in length) to take on board and practise in one's everyday life. This was true in our tours with Roger. Every day we would wait expectantly for our pre-supper, half hour get-together. Although these were never compulsory, rarely was anyone missing! We would discuss together what we had seen that day and what was on our itinerary for the following day, ending with a short talk appropriate to our tour's itinerary and a prayer. On tours when Roger was unavailable others would take his place as co-leader and chaplain. Israel, Egypt, Jordan, Greece, Turkey, Malta and Rome were our destinations, re-visiting the Holy Land a number of times. They proved to be much valued and enjoyed with a number of long-lasting friendships made. A nucleus of folk became true pilgrims, joining most of the tours.

A number of pilgrims, including chaplains and co-leaders, have contributed to this book, writing briefly on their memories and experiences and can be read in this Addendum.

Turkey with the Revd Gavin McGrath (Chaplain)

Gavin writes:

Wendy's been a tireless and an intrepid traveller. Nothing rattles her, and being with her on the road can, sometimes, be scary! I recall accompanying Wendy on a group tour she led a few years ago to 'The Seven Churches in Asia'. The flight from London Gatwick to Istanbul in Turkey was misleadingly uneventful!

Our group, many of whom had been on previous tours with Wendy, were seasoned travellers. So, while I was perplexed by the signs in the Istanbul terminal showing where to go to declare 'weapons transport', my companions hardly noticed. We were rushing to gather outside the terminal building where our coach and tour guide would meet us— as Wendy had arranged. The thing was: as our little band of British pilgrims assembled outside the terminal building, no coach was awaiting us nor tour guide welcoming us. Not to worry, however; Wendy had a telephone number to ring. So, with mobile in hand, Wendy began her work 'to get to the bottom of this mess,' as she put it to me in an aside.

Normally standing outside, say, Sevenoaks Railway Station with your luggage while ringing someone at an office nearby isn't a challenge. The snag comes when the said caller (Wendy) does not speak a word of Turkish and the said office does not speak a word of English. But Wendy persisted (speaking slowly and with a tone similar to a school mistress). We learned the coach and tour guide were waiting for us. They just were many miles away in the older international Istanbul airport in Europe and not in the new terminal in Asia where we had landed.

Wendy was eventually informed by an English-speaking person an alternate coach would 'soon' be with us and take us to the original coach. We would likewise meet our tour guide. Meantime Wendy went from person to person, issuing words of assurance and promise. At last, a substitute coach arrived but no accompanying guide. Through a combination of sign language and pigeon-English, the coach driver and Wendy agreed with one another that the best thing was for us to load our luggage onto the coach and board and make for our hotel.

The coach driver was a diminutive chap. Whether it was due to his lack of English or our lack of Turkish or a cigarette embedded in the corner of his mouth, he spoke not a word to us. But what he lacked in communication he more than made up for in his sudden and speedy acceleration out of the airport terminal! You may wonder if it is possible for a large coach, laden with passengers and their luggage, to 'lay rubber' as the tyres screech but our taciturn driver was giving it his best efforts. We were on the road at last.

Our coach driver might have been taking a Lewis Hamilton correspondence course. Our coach barrelled along the Turkish motorway, shifting from left lane to right lane (and someplace in between) at a fast speed in the Turkish rush hour. What added to Wendy's and my concern (as we were both seated directly behind the driver) was his constant conversation on his mobile phone with someone back at the office. With one hand on the steering wheel and one hand holding his mobile, he was engaged in a rather heated conversation while manoeuvring his trusty steed (our coach) around slower motorway traffic. His additional skill was how he kept that one cigarette in his mouth all the time—the cigarette ash never fell!

At one poignant moment—as I saw my life flash past in front of my eyes—Wendy whispered to me, 'This is entirely unprofessional and not what we agreed to in our travel arrangements. I am going to make a formal complaint!' That's when my epiphany occurred: when our lives hung in the balance due to the crazy driving of a Turkish leprechaun, Wendy wasn't humming to herself 'The Day Thou Gavest Lord is Ended', she was fearlessly preparing to make an official complaint! She was upset about things not being done the 'proper way'! We eventually made it to our rendezvous where our original tour guide was waiting for us.

I don't know if Wendy ever received any official acknowledgement of 'unprofessional practice' from the local tour company. On the other hand, she showed me something that bizarre evening on a Turkish motorway: I saw in her what it means to be a tireless and an intrepid traveller.

Gavin continues on a more serious note: Wendy arranged this travel tour to visit some of the church sites mentioned in the New Testament—notably in the Book of Revelation. In the early chapters of the book, the Lord Jesus Christ instructs John to address seven particular churches in Asia Minor. Their problems and challenges are both particular to them and universal. Equally, the warnings, encouragements and hope Jesus gives to these individual churches are an example for all generations of Christians throughout all history.

So, first, visiting these locations in Revelation 'earths' scripture. Standing in the ruins of Laodicea or seeing with one's own eyes the altars of Roman emperors in ancient Ephesus is not simply 'history coming alive' but visible and tangible references to God's actions—actions which are not detached from reality and actual human affairs but rooted in real events and history.

Second, the significant benefit of travelling to Turkey helped me and the others with us to read the Book of Revelation from a larger perspective. After visiting these sites, those of us who were on this tour now read or hear Jesus's words remembering the warmth of the Turkish sun or the brown colours of the landscape or the views out to the Mediterranean Sea—all of which helpfully remind us we are not central characters in the Bible story, but we are only those included in a worldwide and universal people. Travel helps widen our horizons and opens our eyes.

Third, the tours Wendy arranged were more than holidays filled with different sites, food and experiences, but held out the possibility of something quietly profound. For me, it was visiting the purported burial site of the Apostle John at the Basilica of St John in Selcuk, a short walk from ancient Ephesus. The tomb itself is arrestingly modest: it is a simple stone marker. But as I looked down at the marker and then up and around me of the ruins of the sixth century Basilica and then farther out towards the hills around Ephesus and out to the sea, I experienced an almost inexpressible kind of grateful awe. I was seeing hills and views that the Apostle John would have seen, standing in an area where he would have walked. The awe I sensed, however, was more significant: the modesty of the burial marker of the Apostle John fittingly pointed away from John towards the Saviour whom he touched, travelled with, ate with, saw crucified on a Roman cross in Jerusalem and greeted in that empty upper room on Easter Sunday. Although I was merely a twenty-first-century tourist, the one to whom John witnessed as his Lord and Saviour is the very same Lord and Saviour every person can know, serve and love.

Finally, being on this tour was a great opportunity to meet new people and spend time over a coffee, a meal or walking together in busy Istanbul or along an undulating footpath up to see the remains of ancient Colossae. Different ages, temperaments, interests, and backgrounds: but we had fun together.

Turkey with Roger Clarke

Roger writes:

This tour with Wendy to Turkey was to visit first Istanbul and then to go further south to visit the sites of the seven churches as revealed to us in the Book of Revelation.

About 20 of us flew with Wendy to Turkey in October 2015, spending a few days in Istanbul and then travelling south to visit the sites of the seven churches who were written to in the first chapter of Revelation. This tour was particularly memorable for me as it was my first tour with Wendy, having been widowed a year earlier.

The highlights of the tour for me were the amazing warmth and helpfulness shown by my fellow travellers, Wendy's passion for getting the arrangements right and her age-defying energy! I was over-awed by the Hagia Sofia in Istanbul, built as a Christian cathedral in just five years in the sixth century and containing the world's largest interior space at that time and some beautiful mosaics.

At each site of the seven churches Gavin read the corresponding letter and it brought to life our Christian forerunners and their varying struggles at that time. Each evening Gavin led a time of shared reflection, which was very helpful. I was moved when standing in Thyatira to learn it was the centre of the purple dye industry from where Lydia had travelled to Philippi to sell her cloth. At one point Gavin realised we were close to Colossae, now an unexcavated hill; Wendy was determined to go to the top and several of us helped carry her up and down! There were several poignant moments in Ephesus—the marketplace where Paul and John had trodden, a simple communion next to Mary's house and St John's Basilica

Hagia Sofia image (hand painted by Roger Clark, a contributor)

with its baptisteries and the reputed burial place of John—a very special place. In Smyrna (Izmir) again it was the stories of early Christians I remember most: of Polycarp the bishop who was a disciple of John and was martyred there.

On the tour many of the buildings and sites were very impressive, but my abiding memory is the lives of early Christians and the kindness of my fellow travellers: this is the real church as addressed in Revelation.

Israel with Christopher Tucker (co-leader)

It was at the eleventh hour, when Roger Curl told me that due to concern of his mother's health, he would be unable to co-lead our tour to Israel, that I asked Chris to stand in. He was a pastor in Devon and in God's providence he was available.

Chris writes:

It was in 1997 that Wendy asked me if I would be willing and able to step in at very short notice as co-leader to the tour to Israel.

At that time, I was working in a full-time leadership capacity for a local church and so had some degree of flexibility in taking time out. I was familiar with Israel as two years previously I had co-led a group from my own church on a ten-day trip to that land. Additionally, as a young man I had spent 12 months living and working as part of a Christian group based on kibbutzim in the north of the land near the

Golan Heights and Lebanese border. Nevertheless, I was filled with a certain degree of trepidation as I was unfamiliar with my fellow travellers and not accustomed to leading such tours. I need not have worried, however, as the group were most appreciative of my willingness to step in at such short notice and were supportive and encouraging throughout.

Our trip was focused around two central locations. The first part of the tour was based in and around Jerusalem, staying in the guest house on Kibbutz Ramat Rachel. This is located in west Jerusalem just over two and a half miles from the centre of Jerusalem, in the direction of Bethlehem, and so provided an ideal location for exploring Jerusalem and its environs. It also provided an opportunity for the group to get a glimpse into the way of life on a kibbutz as it was at that time. The guest house was extremely comfortable and as one would expect at a kibbutz, mealtimes were characterised by a plentiful supply of food and a variety to please almost every palate. Our time there was spent visiting the Mount of Olives, exploring the Via Dolorosa, taking in the Western Wall and the Temple Mount and negotiating the inevitable crowds at the Church of the Holy Sepulchre as well as sensing the relative peace of Gethsemane. Due to political unrest and in the interest of our safety we were unable to visit Bethlehem and its famous Church of the Nativity.

Almost certainly though the two 'stand-out' visits during this part of the tour stood in stark contrast to one another. Time spent at the Garden Tomb and the opportunity to participate in a communion service there afforded the group the opportunity to rejoice together in their collective experience of the resurrected Christ. By way of complete contrast, time spent in the Jewish Holocaust Museum at Yad Vashem created the space for the group to soberly reflect upon the death of millions of Jews at the hands of the Nazis during the 1930s and 40s.

The second half of the tour was based in the Galilee; we stayed at the Ramot Resort Hotel above the eastern shore of the Sea of Galilee, a location that afforded spectacular views out across the lake towards Tiberias and other lakeside settlements. Once again, the accommodation was to a very high standard and our location made it easy to explore the significant sites of Jewish and Christian interest located in Galilee. Visits were made to Nazareth, Capernaum, Tabgha and a range of other locations of significance to the Christian. Throughout the tour our local guide, together with the coach driver, proved to be a continual source of interesting information and facts concerning the geography and history of the land from ancient times right up to the present day, as well as providing invaluable cultural and occasional political insights. In addition, he constantly endeavoured to ensure the comfort and safety for all members of our party.

For my own part, I never tire of the sights, sounds and smells of the Old City of Jerusalem, but I think the majority of the group preferred the peace and tranquillity of Galilee and found it easier to envisage scenes from the Biblical narrative there. A highlight for everyone though was sharing together in a communion service on a beach on the shores of the lake itself, and as we did so it was not difficult to picture Jesus sharing fish and bread with His first disciples in a similar location.

As I recall, everyone in the group found that being able to hear some of the Old and New Testament accounts read in the actual locations in which they happened often opened up a whole new insight into the passage. In addition, it was always a blessing to be able to gather as a group after our evening meal to reflect on the day and share together in prayer and worship, as well as read and reflect on God's word. Towards the end of our stay, we had an extended time of light-hearted fellowship in which various members of the group participated with their various 'party pieces'.

Thankfully, it is certainly not necessary to visit Israel in order to understand the Bible, or to effectively follow the teachings of Jesus and be his disciple. I know that every member of the group, not least myself, returned from the tour with new insights into the scriptures, running right through from Genesis to Revelation, and for that we were all grateful.

Anne Clarke writes:

Living Israel, 16 to 25 May 2000. This was my first trip to Israel, and I wanted to go with a group of Christians, as a pilgrimage. Later in the year I was going on a secular tour of Israel, and I knew it would be different. How glad I was to do it this way as I was able to put more into my later tour with the knowledge I had gained from the Billington Travel tour.

We were led by Reverend John Wallis, a Bible teacher. As we visited Biblical sites, the scriptures came alive as we were seeing the places where events happened. Some are now very touristy but others, like the Garden Tomb and the Sea of Galilee, and many parts of Jerusalem, took one back to the Bible scenes.

A particular event that I will never forget was the communion service by the Sea of Galilee. It was a very moving service which began by John washing our feet.

Peter Coling writes:

This was the first of many adventures with Wendy as our leader. Never having previously travelled to Israel it really was a remarkable experience. So many place names, familiar to me from the Bible, came to life. Over the centuries some have been over developed and it was difficult to imagine how they might have been in the time of Jesus.

For me the exceptions were Jerusalem and the Sea of Galilee. To enter through one of the gateways into the old city of Jerusalem is akin to stepping into another word, with its narrow streets, ancient buildings and tiny shops, combined with all the hustle and bustle of the crowds. To walk in the footsteps of Christ along the stations of the Via Dolorosa is extraordinary and will stay with me for ever. Likewise, taking a boat and venturing onto the Sea of Galilee is a remarkable experience and it is easy to picture how it was in the time of Jesus.

Greece

Heather Brown writes:

Having been on many of Wendy's excellent, well-organised trips, I was excited to hear she was planning a series entitled 'In the steps of St Paul'. The first of these was a visit to Greece.

A delightful group set off for Thessaloniki in October 2014. We toured the ancient sites in Thessaloniki and saw the beautiful gold artefacts in Vergina, followed by a visit to Philippi to see where Paul had been imprisoned. What a joy it was to have a Christian guide, Voula, who as she read the relevant Bible verses was able to deepen our understanding at each site.

We then flew to Athens, visiting the Acropolis, Mars Hill and many other relevant places. A full day in Corinth was another highlight.

Wendy had carefully chosen all the hotels we stayed in. In Athens the restaurant was on top of the building giving us a 360° view of the city, which thrilled us all.

Each evening we would gather for a time of worship and reflection with inspiring studies led by the Reverend Roger Curl.

What a memorable time it was and so enjoyed by us all.

Pam Coling writes:

Having joined Wendy's group on previous tours, my husband and I had high expectations. We were not disappointed!

Following in the steps of St Paul in Greece opened our eyes to the historical context of his ministry and helped us to understand the way our Christian faith has developed over the centuries.

One of the great delights for me was exploring this ancient country with fellow Christians and sharing the many experiences that Wendy had included in the tour— historical, cultural and social. A communion service beside the stream where Paul gained his first converts was incredibly special. So many faith affirming and treasured memories: visiting Mars Hill, Corinth and the ancient Greek tombs near Thessaloniki, the ancient Olympic stadium and the sight of the floodlit Acropolis and Parthenon.

Time together sharing the 'thought for the day' gave us valuable space for deeper reflection but it was the experience of learning and enjoying fellowship with other believers that made a unique difference to my life.

Revd Dr Roger Curl serving communion by
a stream on the outskirts of Philippi

The Parthenon on a particularly hot day in late spring

Corinth Canal

Jordan

Guy Powell writes:

In April 2017 I went on holiday to Jordan organised and led by Wendy Billington and Reverend Roger Curl.

It was my first holiday on my own following the death of my wife Lesley in 2016 so I was a little apprehensive.

Fortunately, the group who went were folk I had known previously as well as some friends I had known for many years so I felt comforted and comfortable in their company.

I think Jordan was my favourite holiday destination to date. We flew into Amman and in the following days travelled around the country visiting Jeresh, the extensive remains of a Roman city, Karak, a Crusader castle, Petra (the jewel of the holiday) the desert of Wadi Rum where we spent the night in a Bedouin camp, the Dead Sea, back to Amman and a visit to the River Jordan, Mount Nebo and a tour of Amman itself before flying home the next day.

Jordan desert

Malta with Brigadier Ian Dobbie (Chaplain)

Ian writes:

It was inevitable that I should be aware of Malta early in life as my grandfather was governor during the first two years of the siege from 1940 to 1942, when it was awarded the George Cross. On retiring from the army, I was often asked to lecture on the siege during those two years or provide a biographical talk on my grandfather, who had had a most distinguished military career and who was a prominent Christian figure nationally. Some of my credibility was questionable as I had never visited the island; so in 1997 I went there for a long weekend. I returned somewhat disappointed. Although Valetta Harbour was impressive, the museums were rundown with dust prominent, and whereas the Maltese Cross was still displayed with pride, this was not the case with the George Cross.

When Wendy Billington asked me to join her party in 2018, she no doubt found me somewhat lacking in enthusiasm to return, but she has strong powers of persuasion and I am so glad that I succumbed. Apart from benefitting from being a member of a well-administered holiday party and valuing Roger Curl's ministry in the evenings, it was evident that a considerable amount of European money had been invested in the island in recent years. The infrastructure had benefited considerably and the museums were now on a par with those in London. The tunnels in the Limestone Rock which had protected the wartime population so successfully—only one person in 200 was killed in spite of over 2,000 air raids during my grandfather's watch!—were especially well preserved. Additionally trips to Gozo, the San Anton Palace, the beach where the apostle Paul is believed to have landed and a memorable sail around Valetta Harbour all contributed to an attractive and worthwhile holiday. I know that Wendy's other clients will have enjoyed themselves as much as I did.

Malta

Reverend Dr Roger Curl (Chaplain to most tours)

Young Heroes—Syria

Ghayeth Nadour was our guide in Syria. I and Wendy were part of a group of 12 on a short visit to become familiar with the country, each with a view of taking our own groups there. Our guide was only 19, and a perfect young gentleman. A member of the Syrian Orthodox Church, he told me he attended a Protestant Bible school in his spare time, so he could get to know the Bible better.

On one occasion he accidentally said 'Elijah' when he meant 'John the Baptist'. 'No!' interrupted an elderly priest in our party. 'That's wrong!'

'I do my best,' replied Ghayeth, 'and I'm trying to learn more all the time.'

On another day Ghayeth told us he would not be able to join us: his friend had had a serious road accident and he was going to give blood to him.

Where is he now? In the horrors which have happened since those days he will certainly have been conscripted into the army... But I look forward to meeting him again one day when wars and accidents are over.

On the same trip we visited an Orthodox church up in the mountains. A baby was to be baptised. The font looked like a huge cauldron and clouds of steam were rising from it (it was very cold, and the water had been warmed). The Book of Common Prayer says, 'The priest shall take the child and dip it in the water...' But on this occasion, it looked as if they were going to boil 'it'—not surprisingly, the baby screamed the place down.

An Embarrassing Moment, Commemorated in Verse—Turkey

One of the sights of Ephesus is the ancient Public Convenience. It is a marvellous construction, now in ruins, but its original purpose in providing Ephesian worthies with what modern guides call a 'comfort stop' is obvious. Hygiene was maintained by diverting a watercourse so that it continually cleansed the installations. However, the ravages of time have destroyed the noble edifice which housed the facilities, so that a row of comfortable stone-built 'thrones' now stands by the roadside.

When we arrived there and were invited to sit down, all our party promptly took seats on the jagged rocks on the other side of the road. This prompted me to compose the following:

On my travels I've been,
and with wonder have seen
Many sights to amaze and bemuse.
But, though marvels abound,
In no place have I found
Aught to match the Ephesian loos.

'Tis a wonderful show,
All the seats in a row,
In convivial proximity placed.

And be not offended,
For all is intended
To give no offence to good taste.

The fragrance is sweet,
For just under the seat
The rivulet courses along.
No need here for Jeyes,
Dettol, Airwick or Haze,
There's never a niff nor a pong.

But the centuries have flown,
And with vigour well known
The English are 'doing the town'.
The temperature's baking,
Their limbs all are aching,
And they need a good place to sit down.

But their breeding is fine,
And no matter their pain,
To their English propriety they hold.
They steadfastly refuse
To sit ON the loos,
Even though they're two thousand years old.

Such things are not done,
So, alas, to each one
This 'stop' brings no 'comfort' at all.
To their guide they attend,
From beginning to end,
Primly perched on the OPPOSITE wall.

Ancient Greek Latrine

An Embarrassing Moment, Averted—Egypt

Many of our Muslim friends are very particular about 'modesty'—no shorts for men and no bare arms and shoulders for the ladies when they visit 'holy' places. The monks who attend the Christian shrines are the fussiest of all. As we were arriving at St Catherine's Monastery on Mount Sinai a coach-load of Americans drew up ahead of us. We couldn't but notice that one of their party was a bronzed young lady wearing a two-piece swimming costume, which was the same colour as her skin, and looked as if she was...

A fury of gesticulating and chattering in Arabic broke out amongst the monks at the door. One of them ran inside and emerged with a large cloak. He and a colleague approached the young lady, one on each side, and enveloped her!

My Most Embarrassing Moment—Israel

Jacob was one of the most knowledgeable guides we ever had and unfortunately one of the rudest! He was a veteran of the Israeli Army and seemed unaware that we were not a bunch of his young squaddies.

The next year we went back. In the arrivals lounge at Tel Aviv airport one member who had been with us the previous year asked, 'Who's our guide? Is it Jacob?'

'No way!' I answered, 'he was so RUDE!'

A tap on my shoulder, I turned round and who should it be?

'How good to hear you praising me!' Jacob, now working for airport security, had seen me from the other side of the hall and had beamed in with his listening device. My granny used to say, 'Listeners hear no good of themselves.' But I suspect there was a kind heart under the gruff exterior, and that he would have been brilliant if some emergency had arisen.

The Worst Meal I Have Ever Eaten—Rome

...was in the pizzeria of our hotel in Rome. I'd had a delicious meal there earlier in the week, so we took our party there with high expectations. The pizzas, when they arrived, were topped with something that looked like bacon rinds or pork scratching. Still, I thought, there's always the dessert... It was a pizza base with melted chocolate poured on it.

A friend who used to run a transport I told me that the lorry drivers would throw the food at him if it was not up to standard. I was tempted...

'O Sabbath rest by Galilee'

When I lived in Liverpool in the early 1970s there were no smoke-control laws in force. When you opened the door in the morning the smoke from the nearby power station and dozens of domestic chimneys mingled with the stink of diesel and, hanging on the fog from the Mersey, would provoke a fit of coughing. The scene changes to Galilee on a spring morning. The lake was blue, the hills were green, and all was fresh and beautiful in the sunlight. 'It's been worth living to have come here,' said a dear old lady who taught in Sunday school. 'You can just picture Jesus walking around here!'

True enough—but the Galilee where he walked would have been more like Liverpool. It was a heavy industrial area with the stink of dozens of fish-curing works, the dye-works at Magdala, the tanneries, etc.

But of course, it was into this world with all its ugliness and dirt that he came—and it was because of OUR ugliness and dirt that he died and rose again.

Greece

When we visited the ruins of Corinth our guide showed us an inscription on an ancient pavement: 'Erastus pro adelitate sua pecunia stravit' (Erastus, when he left office, had the pavement laid at his own expense).

We learn from Acts that Erastus was the city treasurer. But what did he do when he left office? Having become a Christian believer when Paul visited his city, he became one of Paul's assistants and travelled with him.

But he never forgot his friends in Corinth and, it seems, he came back there regularly. And when he left the office he paid for the pavement as a parting gift, as if he wanted to say, 'Here's a present for you all. Thanks for everything. Time to move on.' And because of the events which occurred in the Bible lands, we can all leave this world as Erastus left Corinth—with gratitude to God and to our fellow men and women, at peace, and full of expectation of what is in store on the journey we are about to begin.

I am grateful to Wendy for giving me the privilege of helping many friends to learn about these lands and the wonderful things which happened there.

The proud father of his newly born daughter he called
'Wend' using Wendy when she was naughty!

Wendy aged ten in Brownie uniform

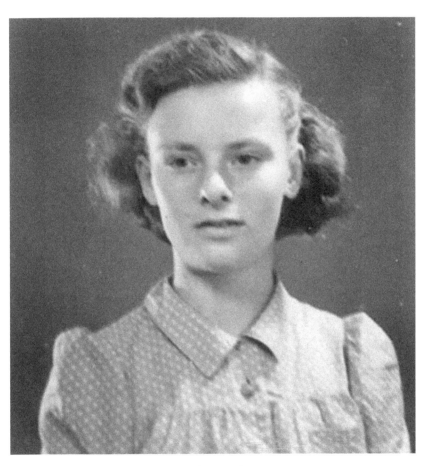
Wendy aged 14

Wendy aged 21

Wendy in her early thirties

Wendy aged 90

Mary and Wendy with their parents Taffy and Ruby.
In the centre is Ruby's school friend Olive who moved
to New York at the start of WW2.

Mary, Wendy's sister and husband Hugh

Wendy seated with Mary and Hugh. Standing behind
are their sons with their wives and four grandchildren

Milton Keynes UK
Ingram Content Group UK Ltd.
UKHW022023221023
431136UK00009B/26

9 781803 816241